SPICES

sophie grigson

SPICES

photography by david loftus

Quadrille
PUBLISHING

contents

*To all at the Summertown Wine Café – owners, staff and customers,
who have nurtured me while I wrote this book. Good coffee, good wine,
laughter and a warm welcome. Thank you.*

Cook's notes

The recipes in this book have all been tested in my kitchen, but please bear
in mind as you cook that recipes are guidelines, not immovable formulae.
Ingredients vary more than you might imagine, from brand to brand, batch
to batch, and so too do saucepans, ovens and hobs. It's important when you
prep and cook to use all your senses if you want to get the best results. Be
aware that cooking times are approximate guides, and use your experience
and common sense to judge when dishes are cooked.

Serving quantities are approximate too. If dishes are to be part of a big
meal, they will feed more people, but when they are to be eaten by a gang
of hungry teenage boys you will probably have to cook double.

Please note the following:
• I always use large free-range eggs in the recipes
• Spoon measurements are rounded, unless otherwise stated
• I use a 5ml teaspoon and a 15ml tablespoon
• Herbs are fresh unless otherwise stated
• Cooking times are approximate

As a cook, I grab a jar of cumin, or a pinch of chilli, or a teaspoon of warm-scented cinnamon with barely a thought of where it came from, its history or even how it was grown. Spices are so familiar that much of the time we ignore their provenance, accepting their scent as our due, then shutting them back in the cupboard until we need them again. How curious, then, that they have not only found their way into the heart of homes across the entire globe, but have also changed the lives of kings, queens, governments and nations. Spices carry within them an unparalleled magic, one that inspires greed, lust, romance, nostalgia and perhaps most importantly of all, the power to enthral cooks and consumers alike.

Whilst writing this book, I have discovered so much that I didn't know about spices. In some cases it has been new ways to get the best out of them, with others magnificent stories they have gathered over the centuries. I know far more about science than I did a few months ago, and far more about complete claptrap.

One thread that has wound its way consistently through the book is a desire to find out what spices really are. How are these small balls of rusty brown and black grown? What plants do the seeds and their pods come from, and where do they thrive? The answers are extraordinarily varied, with some spices plucked from shady trees, others pulled from ground-hugging tangled stems and a fair few unearthed from hard, parched soil.

Some spices are more exotic than others. Plantations in hot, tropical islands are inevitably more romantic than wide fields, harvested by machine, in temperate climes. Some, like pepper, nutmeg and cloves, have radically changed the course of world history, while others have simply melded into daily lives and daily meals without fanfare.

In this book I've concentrated on my favourite spices. Each one has its own particular story, just as it has its own particular scent and magic. Each story is as valuable and special as the spice itself.

Sophie

April, 2011

spice
essentials

Every spice has its own individual quirks and demands, but there are a few guidelines and simple techniques that are common to all, or at least most, spices. From buying to frying, these are the basics that every spice cook needs to know.

What is a spice?

The obvious answer, the one that works in most instances, is that spices are the aromatic, edible dried fruits, seeds, stems and roots of plants. As well as enhancing our food, they often have medicinal properties, and they keep for aeons without need for refrigeration. So what about spices that we use both fresh and dried? Is fresh ginger root a spice? Are dried garlic granules a spice? What about lemongrass, a stem that is often dried? My instinct says that ginger is a spice, dried garlic (which I don't care to use much) isn't, and nor is lemongrass, which loses its lustre when dehydrated. Perhaps that's it – a spice is a spice only if it retains its value when dried.

Sourcing spices

Supermarket spices are solid, safe and reliable. They are also limited in range and comparatively highly priced. Most Asian, Middle Eastern and West Indian food shops are marvellous spice caverns, with shelves stacked full of tempting packets, some holding familiar spices, others stuffed with unknown brown- and rust-coloured powders. Here you will get impressive deals on spices of all sizes and shapes. If you are lucky, you may also end up taking home spices of undiminished vibrancy. Reduced processing can mean bigger flavour. Unfortunately there's a brace of pitfalls. The first is that there are fewer guarantees of quality, so look carefully at what you buy. The second is that you may have to buy in larger quantity than you really need.

A third source is the sweet-scented spice markets that you visit when you travel in spice-producing countries. Here you have to be very, very careful. If you can befriend a local to shop with you, so much the better. Insist on sniffing and, where reasonable, tasting spices before handing over your money. Bargain hard if prices seem high but remember that sometimes alluring low-cost spices may not be all they're cracked up to be.

The internet is a good starting point for sourcing spices, both household names and the ones that local shops do not stock (see page 219). Plan ahead and you should get exactly what you want.

What to buy

The sheer, gorgeous magic of spices lies predominantly in the essential oils they contain. An essential oil is a concentrated volatile oil that carries the characteristic scent of the plant it comes from. Volatility, in other words the tendency to evaporate swiftly, is both a gift and a curse. It means that as we grind spices, their aroma is released, perfuming the air around us and the food it is added to. This is why the human race has always fallen under the spell of spices, since time immemorial.

The downside is that these beautiful-smelling oils don't hang around for long once they are unleashed. The art of cooking with spices is capturing their essence before it flees into the ether, dissipating and disappearing almost without trace.

In order to do this, you will need to buy whole spices wherever possible, and grind them only when you need them. It's easy enough to do (see page 13). Whole spices guard the essential oils inside, and they last almost indefinitely if stored properly. The hoards of spices found in Tutankhamun's tomb are proof enough of that, retaining traces of the scents that made them necessary for his journey to the after-life over 3,000 years ago.

Although buying ready ground spices may seem the easier option, in the longer term you lose out. Each time you open the lid an invisible cloud of aroma escapes, reducing the potency of the powdered spice inside. After three or four uses it will have already paled to a shadow of its former proud self. Soon there is nothing for it but to throw out what's left, unless you are willing to put up with the dull, lifeless traces of scent left behind. What's the point of that?

As ever, there are exceptions, or rather the occasional lack of option. The three most obvious instances are cinnamon, ginger and turmeric. Whole cinnamon sticks are hard to grind to a fine powder, so it makes sense to lay in a small stock of ground cinnamon. Luckily, this is a spice you are likely to use up fairly quickly in sweet dishes as well as savoury. Similarly, whole chunks of dried ginger are rock-like, making ground ginger welcome for baking or in Moroccan recipes. Replace it regularly if you don't want your ginger nuts to lose their snap. Although it is possible to track down fresh or dried whole turmeric, it's not so easy. Again, buy it ground, change it often.

Whatever the state of the spices you buy, the mantra has to be: buy little, buy often.

How to store spices

Bin the spice rack. Sorry, but it has got to go. The wall or counter-top spice rack is pretty much the worst place in the kitchen to store your spices. It may be neat and orderly, but light and heat are spices' worst enemies, especially ground spices; they sap the flavour, and bleach out colour. Make space in a kitchen cupboard, or better still, a drawer where spices will be shielded from light and the extra warmth it brings. The very best place is probably the fridge, but for most of us that is totally impractical. Fridges, like handbags, are never big enough for everything we have to squeeze into them. Piling in twenty-something spice jars is a non-starter.

Most of my spices nestle cosily in a kitchen drawer, a system that works particularly well since I persuaded (okay, bribed) my children to label the lids clearly one dull rainy afternoon. Now I can see at a glance which is which. No more rifling through the cereal packets and jams pots in the cupboard, that deliberately hide the one spice I need.

Keep individual spices in small airtight jars. Glass is good but metal and plastic are fine too. Double check that the seal is tight, to lock volatile oils inside the jar, and keep moisture out. Spices don't appreciate damp, either.

You'll find a masala dabba, a metal spice box, in most Indian kitchens. The tin contains a number of smaller metal containers for spices. A traditional masala dabba has two lids: an inner one that sits neatly over the spices and can be lifted on and off easily; and a main lid that fits the box snugly and seals it properly when not in use. It works well in households where spiced dishes are eaten day in day out all year round, but where this isn't the case, westernised masala dabbas with individual lids for each spice are a better option. Use a spice box to store the spices you use most frequently – cumin, coriander, turmeric, chilli, mustard seed, cinnamon and your own home-made garam masala, perhaps – tailoring it to fit your needs. If you are keen on the masala dabba, you might fill a second one with the sweeter spices used for baking – cinnamon, nutmeg, cloves, cardamom, ground ginger, caraway and saffron.

Either way, if you use a masala dabba, store it as you would spice jars, in a cupboard or drawer, away from light, heat and moisture.

A final point: write the date you first use a spice on the jar. Go through all your spice jars at least once a year and throw out all ground spices that have been open for more than 6 months, and all whole spices that are more than 3 or 4 years old.

PREPARING AND USING SPICES

Dry-frying

Although it is perfectly reasonable and common to use spices raw,
either ready ground, or grinding them yourself to order, most of
the great spice recipes begin with dry-frying whole spices to release
their full inner majesty. The process also takes off some of the
rough rawness, and crisps them up, making them easier to grind.

Dry-frying, roasting, dry-roasting and toasting are all one and the
same thing when it comes to preparing whole spices:

Heat a small or medium frying pan over a medium heat. Add
the whole spices and shake the pan gently and constantly over the
heat until the spices turn a shade or two darker, and release their
fragrance. This will take no more than 3 or 4 minutes. Quickly tip
them into a bowl or mortar (to prevent them cooking any further)
and cool before grinding.

There are a few spices that burn more quickly than others – dried
red chillies, for instance – and these are usually added towards
the end of the dry-frying process. Ground spices such as turmeric
should not be dry-fried.

Bhuna

A bhuna is a curry that takes its name from the widely used bhuna
technique. A spice paste, usually moistened with onion, garlic and
ginger, is fried in oil until all the moisture is driven off, and the
paste starts to brown. It is essential to stir the mixture more or less
constantly, scraping up any bits that stick, so that it cooks evenly.

Frying and tempering

Many spicy Asian recipes begin with frying whole spices, before the
remaining ingredients see the pan. The idea is firstly to bring out
the full cooked scent of the spices, and secondly to flavour the oil
itself, which then carries the taste to the rest of the dish.

Some spices, particularly mustard seeds, burst and bounce in
the heat, leaping exuberantly out of the pan. To save you and your
kitchen from attack, clamp on a lid, or lay a baking sheet over the
pan, just for a few seconds, until the frenzy dies down.

Tempering, or last-minute frying of spices, is another important
technique, used in Indian, Pakistani and Bangladeshi cooking.

To temper spices, heat some oil, or oil and butter in a frying pan, add chopped onion, garlic or ginger if required, and cook for a few minutes, then add whole spices, and fry for another minute or so. The mixture, oil or butter and all, is poured, still sizzling merrily, straight into the main dish. It's an excellent way to improve a lack-lustre soup or stew. This technique is so popular that it has a wealth of different names, tarka or tadka being amongst the most common.

Grinding and grating

I fell in love with my pestle and mortar when I realised where I'd been going wrong for many, many years. If you've ever tried grinding spices to a powder or garlic and ginger to a paste in a mortar, only to have little bits skidding away from the pestle (or pounder), or worse shooting across the kitchen like miniaturised clay pigeons, be reassured: it wasn't your fault, it was the mortar's.

A good mortar has the following qualities: it must be heavy, it must be hard, and the interior surface must be rough. The same goes for the pestle. Smooth, glazed or wooden ones are hopeless. Invest in a weighty cast-iron or stone pestle and mortar and you will discover how wonderful and effective they are to use.

There are two basic motions involved when using a pestle and mortar. Pounding has its uses, particularly for larger chunks of stuff and for crushing extra hard spices, or for crushing very small amounts. A circular grinding motion is often more effective, especially when you are aiming for a fine grind.

When it's very finely ground spices you're after, you'll get a near-perfect result from an electric spice/coffee grinder. There are many to choose from, but you want one with a transparent lid so you can see what's going on inside, a fairly strong motor (170 watts upwards) and one that's easy to clean. A ceramic grinding mechanism is a bonus. If you can't be persuaded that a pestle and mortar is a good thing, you might be wise to invest in a 'Wet & Dry Spice Grinder'. Spices rarely grind properly in a food processor.

For nutmeg, fresh ginger and turmeric a different approach is required. You can buy small nutmeg graters to keep with your nutmeg, but many are too flimsy to be of use. Better by far to purchase a fine Microplane grater or similar hyper-sharp hand-held grater. This is ideal for grating nutmeg, ginger or turmeric, not to mention lemon or orange zest and Parmesan.

The Japanese make beautiful ergonomic ginger graters, but the one I was given lies lonely and dusty in a cupboard. In most modern kitchens equipment has to multi-task, and that ginger grater didn't.

mustard
seed

chillies

paprika

pepper

hot spices

Chillies, chillies everywhere and even in the drink – chilli vodka and chilli beer for a start. They are so very fashionable, so hugely variable, so endlessly complicated, so bemusing and yet so thrillingly simple. They've even spawned a brand new word, the chilli-head: a person, usually but by no means exclusively male, who just can't get enough of that chilli heat. A man who yearns to show that he is tough and brave (or foolish) enough to munch his way through half a dozen volcanic habanero chilli peppers, or better still, Naga chillies, currently considered the hottest in the world.

chillies

Habaneros (so closely related to Scotch bonnet that for all practical purposes they are the same) rate a staggering 100,000–350,000 units on the Scoville Heat Scale, while the epic Nagas race ahead with 1 million units or more. Wilbur Scoville created the scale in 1912. He developed a method of extracting the capsaicin (the substance that makes chilli peppers hot), diluting it with a sugar solution, then persuading a band of volunteers to rate the heat accordingly. A chilli-head's dream job, but sadly they hadn't been invented then.

These days, though Scoville units are still quoted, a more accurate measurement of heat can be obtained using liquid chromatography. Scoville units are old hat, having been replaced by ASTA (American Spice Trade Association) pungency units. Bottom of both scales is the sweet bell pepper (score 0), although it hardly counts as a chilli.

Not only do chillies vary drastically in ASTA pungency units, but also in taste, colour, shape and size. There are hundreds of them, literally. But they all started off in the same spot. South America is the place we have to thank for the world's most popular spice. Ecuador currently holds the record for the oldest archeological remains of chilli peppers. Modern techniques have made it possible to analyse fossilised starch grains found in remote sites and prove that they are from chillies over 6,000 years old.

By the time Europeans stumbled over the Americas on the hunt for Asia, chillies were a common domesticated plant on the continent. Once again Colombus and his cohorts, desperate to find a good source of black pepper, named them peppers (or rather pimento in Spanish), a name that has stuck and continues to confuse the unwary.

In fact chillies are all-round confusing. Today there are literally thousands of cultivars. Many of them are pictured on the Chile-Head database at www.g6csy.net/chile – a mind-boggling list of over 3,000 chillies, in full technicolour glory. Tidily they divide into a modest five species or groups. *Capsicum annuum* includes sweet bell peppers, jalapeño and cayenne, while *Capsicum frutescens* takes in Tabasco chillies and the Malagueta variety, which is popular in Brazil. Many of the big hitters, the habanero and Naga for instance, belong to the *Capsicum chinense* clan. In Peru the predominant group is the *Capsicum baccatum*, which includes the delicious citrusy lemon drop chilli. Last and most select is the *Capsicum pubescens* with just a handful of cultivars, all with dark brown/black seeds, best known of which is the Peruvian rocoto chilli.

Equally intriguing is how a small plant from South America conquered much of the rest of the world in little over half a century. It would be remarkable now, but in an era without electricity, telephone or engines, it's extraordinary. Christopher Colombus brought the first chillies back to Europe in 1493, but they didn't take kindly to the climate, and failed to thrive. The Portuguese got their hands on hardier varieties, and carried them wherever they sailed. They introduced chillies to their African colonies, then sailed on round the Cape of Good Hope and on to the Malabar coast in order to fill their holds with black pepper and other spices.

The theory goes that Indians, already used to the heat of black pepper and ginger, instantly appreciated the joys of chillies. What's more, chillies are so much easier to grow than black pepper that everyone could afford to grow or buy them, however poor. Within 50 years, chillies were regular fare. Traders had hauled them along trading routes across the country, through Burma and into China. The Portuguese sailed right on to Japan, sowing capsicum seed wherever they put into harbour. An extraordinary migration, indeed.

The Europeans were far more suspicious of this new plant. For decades they grew chillies purely for their decorative value. Indeed much of Europe has taken a full five centuries to get interested in the potential of the chilli. Early adopters were Hungary and Spain (see Paprika, page 35), and more unexpectedly, the south of Italy where chilli is still an important flavouring.

Chilli, or rather capsaicin, has inevitably made its mark in areas outside the kitchen. Research is continuing to discover whether it may be beneficial in the treatment of prostate and other cancers, but there's little doubt that it can work as an anti-inflammatory. Recently I bought a handsomely packaged 'porous capsicum plaster', which claims to be 'the comfortable remedy for lumbago'. Since I don't suffer from lumbago, its effectiveness is untested for now. ❖

harissa

Makes a 150ml jar

110g medium-hot red chillies, halved and
   deseeded

4 garlic cloves, peeled

1 teaspoon coriander seeds

1 teaspoon cumin seeds

1 teaspoon caraway seeds

2 tablespoons roughly chopped coriander
   leaves

¼ teaspoon salt

4 tablespoons extra virgin olive oil, plus
   extra to seal

Wild, intense and very exciting, this Moroccan chilli relish has to be one of the great
chilli sauces. You can buy it ready made, but your own home-spun version will taste
twice as good. It's traditionally served with couscous, but there's no reason why
you should limit it to Moroccan dishes. Stir a little into a tomato sauce as it cooks,
or into a soup or stew. Make harissa mayonnaise for sandwiches, or add a spoonful
to a shepherd's pie.

Roughly chop the chillies and garlic and place in a food processor.

Dry-fry the whole spices in a small pan over a moderate heat until they turn a shade darker,
scenting the kitchen. Cool, then grind to a powder.

Add the ground spices to the chillies with the chopped coriander and salt. Process until
finely chopped, scraping down the sides a few times. Keep the blades whirring as you
gradually trickle in the olive oil.

Scrape the harissa out into a small screw-top jar. Pour a thin layer of olive oil over the
surface to exclude the air. It will keep for a month or two in the fridge, as long as you make
sure the layer of oil is renewed every time you dip in.

On a less benign note, there is capsaicin's potential as a weapon. The Indian Army has developed a chilli-filled crowd control grenade. The all-powerful bhut jolokia – a Naga-type capsicum known as the ghost chilli – is the key to its effectiveness. And the very same chilli has come to the rescue of farming communities in Assam. Herds of wild elephant frequently trample down crops and homes, but a new approach is promising good results. A searing blend of killer chilli and automobile grease is smeared thickly over jute fences, and the elephants just hate it. So while they turn tail and charge off elsewhere, the villagers cheer and give thanks for the wonderful, explosive heat of the humble chilli.

Types of Chilli

This is an elementary trawl through a handful of the most common chillies, their SHUs (Scoville Heat Units) and other characteristics. It's also worth pointing out that red chillies are simply ripe green chillies. They tend to be hotter, but have a marginally sweeter flavour, which softens the impact.

Jalapeño (SHU 2,500–8,000) This is the classic chilli, enormously widespread, sturdy, easy to grow, and with a good flavour and medium/low heat rating. Sold fresh, red or green, jalapeños are torpedo shaped and around 7cm long. Their thick flesh makes them tricky to dry, but they do take well to pickling and preserving. Pickled jalapeño slices are an excellent store-cupboard item, but not quite as appealing as…

Chipotle (SHU 5,000–10,000) A smoked ripe jalapeño, available dried, pickled or *en adobo* (in a vinegary tomato sauce). Whichever way, chipotles are a real joy if you can get your hands on them.

Fresno (SHU 2,500–10,000) Similar in size and impact to the jalapeño, but with broader shoulders, this is the commonest retail chilli in the UK and Europe. It can be used green or red, usually fresh. It is also known as a Kenyan chilli.

Scotch bonnet and Habanero (SHU 100,000–350,000) These two confederates are so close in flavour and heat that they are totally interchangeable. They look something like a crumpled cube and can be red, orange, yellow or green. They are always used fresh. Scotch bonnets are the chillies of the Caribbean, especially Jamaica. They are outrageously hot, so use them with caution. ➥

baja sauce

Serves 6–8

1 ripe avocado

1 or 2 Fresno or jalapeño chillies, to taste

juice of 1 lime

150ml soured cream

150ml mayonnaise

2 tablespoons chopped coriander leaves

salt

This is a rich, silky sauce for tacos and other Mexican treats. My family love it with practically any barbecued meats or vegetables. Make it as hot or as mild as you fancy, depending on the chilli level of the rest of the food – it even works without any chilli at all.

Halve, peel and stone the avocado and mash the flesh in a bowl. Halve, deseed and chop the chillies, then add to the avocado with the remaining ingredients and beat to combine. Taste and adjust the seasoning before serving.

pico de gallo

Serves 4–6

600g ripe tomatoes

½ red onion, peeled and finely diced

2 garlic cloves, peeled and crushed

3 tablespoons chopped coriander leaves

1 Fresno or jalapeño chilli

juice of 1 lime

salt

Pico de gallo literally means rooster's beak, but it's also the Mexican name for this classic salsa. You can vary it as you like, using spring onions instead of red onion, no chilli, more chilli, replacing some or all of the tomato with mango or avocado and so on. In winter I often make it with quartered cherry tomatoes, which usually have a fuller, sweeter taste than other sad, subdued out-of-season varieties.

Halve, deseed and dice the tomatoes, or quarter cherry tomatoes if using. Place them in a bowl, add all the rest of the ingredients and toss to combine. Leave to stand for at least 10 minutes to allow the flavours to mingle.

Now stir and taste. Adjust the seasonings, adding more lime and/or salt, or a pinch of sugar if the tomatoes need a bit of encouragement. Your salsa is now ready to serve.

fish tacos with pico de gallo

Serves 4

600g haddock fillets (or other firm white
    fish)

½ teaspoon chipotle chilli flakes (or a little
    pickled chipotle, drained and chopped)

juice of 1 lime

2 garlic cloves, peeled and chopped

2 tablespoons extra virgin olive oil

salt and freshly ground black pepper

To serve:

pico de gallo and/or baja sauces (see
    page 21)

2 Little Gem lettuces, shredded

8 corn tortillas

A friend tells me that when she lived in Mexico's Yucatan Peninsular, they'd often go down to the beach to get fish tacos and an ice-cold beer at the end of a hot day. The vendor would hand them deep-fried whole fish and they'd pick the flesh off the bones, pile it into corn tortillas, season with chilli and lime, then roll up and eat. Occasionally they'd get pico de gallo, but not always.

To make my life easier, I use fish fillets, but the principle is the same. As well as the tomato salsa, I like a spoonful or two of cooling baja sauce, but without chillies in it, so that it soothes the heat of the chipotle fish and tomato salsa. It's perfect outdoor food, so if the weather's amenable, I'll cook the fish on the barbecue.

Lay the fish fillets in a dish and sprinkle with the chipotle, lime juice, garlic, olive oil and some salt and pepper. Turn the fillets to coat in the mixture and leave to marinate for at least half an hour. Put the sauce(s), and lettuce into bowls ready to serve.

Line the grill rack with foil and preheat the grill thoroughly. Take the fish from the marinade and place on the grill rack. Grill close to the heat without turning for around 5–6 minutes, until the top browns a little and the fillets are just cooked through.

Meanwhile, heat the tortillas according to packet instructions – either foil-wrapped in the oven or in the microwave.

Quickly break the fish into large flakes. Serve with the hot tortillas and accompaniments, so that all your fellow diners can roll up their own tacos, with a little of the grilled fish, scarlet pico de gallo, soothing baja sauce and crisp sweet lettuce.

Cayenne (SHU 30,000–50,000) This glossy scarlet chilli is slender and long, up to 20cm, tapering to a point. A shot of dried ground cayenne is the easiest way to power up the heat in any dish, but tread cautiously. Be sure to store ground cayenne in a dark cupboard as sunlight bleaches out the bright colour.

Poblano and Ancho (SHU 1,000–1,500) The favourites in Mexican cooking. Poblano chillies are comparatively big, rather like a pointy bell pepper, with a sweet, fruity flavour. When dried they become anchos, which are even nicer. Mulato is a dark variety of ancho.

Bird chilli/Thai chilli/Birds eye chilli (SHU 100,000–225,000) The terms bird and birds eye chilli are used to describe several different chillies, which makes matters tricky. I define them as those small, spindly chillies, 3–5cm long, that pack an enormous punch. They come fresh, red or green, and should be employed with restraint.

Espelette chilli (SHU 4,000) Grown in the French Basque country, around the small town it is named after, the Piment d'Espelette is a relatively mild chilli with a terrific flavour – fruity and complex. It has an AOC, in other words it can only be grown in a specified area. It is used fresh, dried, pickled and ground.

Chilli powder Much of what is sold as chilli powder is barely chilli at all – it may contain a little as 10–20% ground chilli peppers. Aimed at the chilli con carne maker, it will also contain cumin and oregano, possibly with the addition of salt and garlic powder. As a result this is pretty mild stuff. Confusingly, a few brands of chilli powder, usually Asian, are pure chilli. Moral of this story: check for an ingredients list, a sure indication that it is a blend.

Notes on chilli

Which is better, dried or fresh? Neither. They're just different. Fresh chillies have a juicy, light vibrancy, while dried ones have a concentrated, almost caramelised tone that may be more complex. They keep well too, but you can't stuff a dried chilli pepper.

✿ There's no ducking the heat issue; even when armed with a Scoville rating, you never quite know how hot an individual chilli is until you eat it. To me, this is part of the fun. Another is the flavour they bring to a dish, alongside the heat. Incidentally, as a rough rule of thumb, the smaller the chilli the hotter it is. ➥

vietnamese shaking beef

Serves 3–4

500g sirloin steak, trimmed

2–3 tablespoons sunflower, rapeseed
   or vegetable oil

Marinade:

2 tablespoons oyster sauce

1 tablespoon soy sauce

2 teaspoons fish sauce

3 garlic cloves, peeled and crushed

1½ teaspoons caster sugar

Dressing:

juice of 2 limes

2 Fresno or jalapeño chillies, deseeded
   and finely chopped

1 tablespoon caster sugar

1 tablespoon fish sauce

To serve:

75g watercress, trimmed

½ cucumber, cut into batons

100g cherry tomatoes, halved

Is that beef quivering and trembling at the thought of the chillies? Perhaps so, but this dish actually gets its name from the cooking method. In Vietnam it is a celebratory dish, made when times are good. You can play around with the bed of salad under the steaming beef if you like, but bear in mind that the greenery should wilt slightly in the warmth and get bathed in the juices.

A lovely combination if ever there was one...

Cut the beef into 2cm cubes and toss with the marinade ingredients. Set aside to marinate for 30 minutes or so.

Mix the dressing ingredients in a large bowl. Toss the watercress, cucumber and tomatoes together and arrange either on a large serving dish or on individual plates.

Heat half the oil in a wok or large frying pan over a high heat. Add half the beef and spread out into a single layer, then let it cook for 1 minute without moving. Now shake the wok from side to side to turn the cubes and let the beef cook for another minute. Repeat once more, until the beef is toasty brown on the outside. Scoop the beef out and straight into the dressing. Repeat with the remaining meat.

Toss all the meat together in the dressing, then pile it onto the salad, along with all the juices. Serve at once.

✣ There is a widespread belief that the seeds of a chilli are the hottest part. In fact, there is usually a greater concentration of capsaicin in the whitish membranes that attach the seed to the walls. This is the bit to remove if you want to play safe. Other than aesthetic, there is no critical reason to deseed chillies before use.

✣ If you have sensitive skin or you're about to prepare vast quantities of chillies, invest in a pair of thin rubber gloves. Capsaicin can be quite an irritant, even for tough hands. Whether it's a brace of chillies, or a stack, whether you wear gloves or not, take enormous care after preparation. Capsaicin is hard to rinse away (it's not water-soluble), so woe betide you if you rub your eyes, go to the loo, or as I once did, insert contact lenses, before it is all scrubbed away.

✣ On a cheerier note, remember that if you take a mouthful of searingly hot chillied food, the best way to soothe the pain is to take a few good swigs of some kind of alcoholic drink (capsaicin is alcohol-soluble) or dairy-based drink (capsaicin is also soluble in milk products). Water is no more than a very temporary palliative.

Cooking with chillies

Like pepper, chilli goes with practically everything. It's odd that a powerful substance works to enhance rather than mask the flavours of other ingredients. Even delicate fish works beautifully with a touch of chilli, without losing its identity. The same can be said for chicken or steak, cauliflower or tomatoes, melon or chocolate. Yes, chilli with fruit is a winner. On the streets of Thailand vendors sell wedges of juicy mango with little bags of sugar mixed with finely chopped red chilli to dip them into. It's a brilliant combination.

Mexico is home to some of the most fascinating and delicious of chillies, too many to list here, and disappointingly, many available only on their home ground, or by mail order. As a result there's a range of cooking methods that are unfamiliar to other cooks.

Like Mexico every traditional chilli-growing country has a wealth of recipes for curries, stir-fries, stews, salads, dressings, sauces, marinades and more. Modern cooks who have stumbled on chillies more recently have brought new initiatives, some reviving old practices. The best example has to be the recent passion for spicing up chocolate with chilli. It goes right back to the Ancient Aztecs, who greeted Hernando Cortez with a goblet of chillied chocolate... It must have been quite a shock to his taste buds.

sweet heat pineapple jelly

Serves 6–8

1 litre pineapple juice

1 tablespoon caster sugar

1 or 2 dried or fresh red chillies

10 sheets leaf gelatine

1 teaspoon vanilla extract

The shock of chilli in a fruit jelly is thrilling and delicious. Quite how strong you make it is entirely your choice. Taste the juice as it heats and remove the chillies as soon as you think they've done their job.

Set the jelly either in one large mould, or in individual glasses or bowls.

Put the pineapple juice and sugar into a saucepan. If using dried chillies, break them into small pieces; if using fresh, chop them roughly. Add the chilli to the juice in the pan. Heat very slowly, stirring occasionally to dissolve the sugar, until very hot, but not boiling.

Meanwhile (as soon as you put the pan on the hob), half-fill a small roasting tin with cold water and submerge the gelatine leaves in it. Leave to soak and soften.

Taste the pineapple juice. If it is already zinging with chilli heat, remove the chilli pieces. If not, turn the temperature right down low and leave for a few minutes longer.

Now take the perky, steaming pineapple juice off the heat. Stir in the vanilla extract. Take out a couple of the gelatine leaves and squeeze out the water, then drop them into the hot pineapple juice and stir to dissolve. Repeat with the remaining gelatine.

Pour the jelly into mould(s) and leave to cool, then transfer to the fridge to set. Serve with a little pouring cream if you like.

The defensive chemistry of the mustard seed is sly and aggressive. Each tiny little globe, a mere millimetre or two in diameter, looks so very innocent. Indeed if you put it into your mouth, crunch down and then swallow immediately you might well wonder how this can possibly be connected with the mouth-burning yellow mustard paste that goes so very well with rare roast beef.

mustard seed

The answer is isothiocyanates. These are the mustard plant's ordnance. Stored safely in each seed, temporarily inactivated so that they do no damage to the plant itself, they are weapons designed to shock and awe predators. At the first hint of attack, guardian enzymes set to work unleashing the power of the isothiocyanates. Like genies let out of the bottle, they wake up as the cell walls are broken. Growling and snarling, they spew out the violent heat that to us characterises mustard.

In the kitchen – or mustard factory – this means that in order to create table mustard we first have to grind the seeds to a fine powder. Since the seeds are dry and brittle, moisture is also required to set the isothiocyanates back on the warpath. It takes around 10 minutes to detect the heat, and the mixture has little more than an hour of life in it, unless it is stabilised with something acidic – usually a sharp dose of vinegar.

Underneath the fierceness, isothiocyanates are oddly puny. They can't stand the heat. Simmering or roasting anything flavoured with mustard annihilates the pungency, leaving nothing but a mild essence of mustard.

The mustard plant is one of the bossy clan of Brassicas, alongside rape, turnips, cabbages, radishes and broccoli. Like these it grows prolifically in temperate climates all around the world, enjoying moisture and cool weather. Canada is the biggest producer in the world, growing around 90% of the world's crop.

Mustard seeds grow inside a silique, a form of pod divided down the centre by a translucent membrane. As the silique dries out at the end of the growing season, it splits open, throwing seeds to the ground. A clever piece of design from Mother Nature, but a trial for agriculture. Mustard farmers have to keep a keen eye on their crop in order to harvest it when the majority of the seeds are just a minim under ripe. Too green and they won't ripen and dry properly off the plant. A tickle over ripe and they will spill onto the ground at the merest whisper of a breeze.

Many moons ago, when California was first being colonised by the Spanish, mustard was one of the plants that went with the Franciscan priests when they set up their missions. There were 21 Franciscan Missions in all, spread out over 600 miles, and linked by El Camino Real, the Mission Trail running from Sonoma in the north to San Diego in the south. Striding or riding between mission posts in the warm sunshine, the priests scattered mustard seeds on either side of the path to guide and hearten others on the long journey up and down the coast.

Today, the old mission trails are largely obliterated by multi-lane highways, but in the Napa Valley the vineyards burst into yellow flower every January. Are these the descendants of those priestly mustard seeds, run wild over the centuries? Perhaps, but the locals love them whatever. There's even a Mustard Festival to celebrate it.

Types of mustard seed

The three main varieties are white, brown and black.

White (or yellow) mustard seed The mildest of all mustards, *Brassica hirta* or *Sinapis alba* is widely grown. It probably originates from the Southern Mediterranean and is more of a yellowy tan than white. Used for table mustards and whole in pickling spices.

Brown mustard seed More pungent than white, *Brassica juncea* brings a more volcanic bite to table mustards and other dishes where it's used ground. Like white mustard seed it is probably native to the Southern Mediterranean. It features in Asian dishes, and is a suitable replacement for black mustard seeds in recipes. ➥

coarse-grain tarragon honey mustard

Makes two 150ml jars

50g white mustard seeds

50g brown mustard seeds

120–150ml water

2 tablespoons cider vinegar or tarragon
    vinegar

½ tablespoon salt

2 tablespoons honey

leaves from 1 large tarragon sprig

⅛ teaspoon ground turmeric

Making your own mustard is easy and as a bonus you get to choose the flavourings and degree of heat. Tarragon and honey is very good in a sandwich with rare roast beef, but instead you could try adding fresh ginger, or sun-dried tomatoes, or fresh or dried dill. Beer mustard is terrific – just replace the water with a classy pale ale. For a hot, hot, hot mustard, reduce the white mustard seeds, and increase the brown. For a truly incendiary mustard, throw in a couple of red hot chillies. Ouch!

Soak all the mustard seeds in 120ml water in a covered bowl for 24 hours.

Tip the mustard seeds and water into a food processor and process until thick and mustardy. This takes longer than you think it is going to, and you'll need to scrape down the sides regularly.

Leave the mustard to stand for around 15 minutes to allow the heat to develop. If it gets too thick, add a dash more water.

Now add all the remaining ingredients and process again until evenly mixed. Taste cautiously, and add a little more vinegar or honey or turmeric if you think it needs it. The flavours will develop further over the next few hours so don't go overboard.

Spoon the mustard into small jars, tapping them firmly on a wooden board occasionally to expel air bubbles. Seal tightly and store in the fridge. Use within a month.

onion & prune chutney

Makes five 350ml jars

6 large onions, peeled and sliced

6 large garlic cloves, peeled and sliced

2 tablespoons extra virgin olive oil

2 tablespoons white mustard seeds

2 dried red chillies

3 cinnamon sticks

250ml apple balsamic vinegar, or red
    wine vinegar

300g granulated sugar

500g stoned prunes

Just 2 tablespoons of mustard seeds is enough to vastly improve the texture of this dark, sticky chutney. No heat, just a mildly nutty crunchiness entwined in the softness of the onions and prunes.

Put the onions, garlic and olive oil into a large heavy-based pan. Cover and cook over a low heat for around 40 minutes, stirring once or twice, until the onions are very soft and floppy.

Now add all the remaining ingredients, except the prunes, and stir. Carry on cooking, uncovered, over a moderate heat, stirring occasionally, for 30 minutes. Stir in the prunes and keep right on bubbling until the mixture is sticky and jammy, another 20–30 minutes.

Fish out and discard the cinnamon sticks and chillies. Ladle the chutney into sterilised jam jars, seal tightly, label and leave to cool.

Store the chutney in a cool, dark cupboard to mature for a week before using. It will keep for up to a year. Once opened, keep it in the fridge.

Black mustard seed The emperor of mustard seed heat, *Brassica nigra* is the one that brings hell and lightning to table mustards. Unfortunately it is a nightmare to harvest mechanically (the seeds split and shatter), so less and less of it is produced. Although it came originally from Eastern Europe, this particular mustard seed is now strongly associated with Indian cooking.

Using mustard seed

If you want heat from your mustard seeds you must grind them up, moisten them and then later add vinegar to stabilise the mixture. In other words, you must make table mustard, the condiment. It's a surprisingly simple process and open to endless variation.

Mustard seed is a frequent ingredient in all sorts of pickles and preserves. Used whole it brings not a mustardy bite, but a mildly nutty taste and a pleasant nubbly texture. The exception to this is sunshine-yellow piccalilli, which revels in its mustard heat. This is usually imparted by powdered instant mustard flour, but I can see no reason why you shouldn't grind your own seeds, either all white or mixed white and brown, adding a little extra turmeric for colour.

The best way to use mustard seeds, especially brown or black, is to turn to the recipes of India, Pakistan, Sri Lanka and Bangladesh. They are used with particular exuberance in southern Indian cooking – with vegetables, meat, fish, whatever. The technique is to fry the mustard seeds in hot oil until they pop and splutter, giving them a delicious toasty taste (cover with a lid for a few seconds to stop them leaping out), then speedily adding other ingredients so that they don't burn. This is called tempering.

Many Indian dishes, especially dahls, are finished with a tarka, a sizzling slick of fried spices, sometimes with garlic and ginger, and the oil or ghee (or butter but take care not to burn it), poured on just before serving. It's a great way to bring last-minute zip to a dull dish.

Look out too for Bengali dishes that include panch phoron – literally five spices – mustard seeds, fennel seeds, nigella, fenugreek and cumin – used either whole or ground (see page 213).

green bean sabzi

Serves 4

200g green beans

1 sweet potato, peeled

2 tablespoons vegetable or sunflower oil

1 teaspoon brown or black mustard seeds

2 teaspoons cumin seeds

1–2 green chillies, chopped

2 garlic cloves, peeled and chopped

⅛ teaspoon asafoetida

1 tomato, deseeded and diced

¼ teaspoon ground turmeric

salt

An Indian sabzi or sabji is nothing more than a spiced vegetable dish, usually quite homely and very good to eat. This one – made with green beans and orange sweet potato – can be eaten as a light lunch dish, with roti or naan bread and a yoghurt raita to moisten it, or served as a side dish with grilled chicken or lamb chops.

Cut the beans into 2cm lengths. Quarter the sweet potato lengthways and slice it thinly.

Heat the oil in a medium frying pan over a medium-high heat. Add the mustard and cumin seeds. As soon as the mustard seeds start popping, clamp the lid on for a few seconds, to stop them shooting all over the place.

Remove the lid and add the chillies, garlic and asafoetida. Fry for a few seconds, then add the green beans, sweet potato, tomato, turmeric and some salt. Stir well, turn the heat down low, cover and cook for 5–8 minutes. Check that the sweet potato is cooked through, taste and adjust the seasonings, then serve.

Hungarians eat a phenomenal amount of paprika. Conservative estimates put it at around a kilo per person per year, and in the paprika-growing areas that rises to a whopping 4 kilos. Wow. Have you got a half-used jar of paprika idling and dusty at the back of a cupboard? How long has it been there? Shame on you. Paprika-hungry Hungarians would have emptied that jar in a matter of days.

paprika

The two main paprika-producing areas in Hungry are Kalocsa and Szeged. During the paprika pepper harvest the area is awash with brilliant scarlet. The fields are a sea of red and green, while the houses are festooned with garlands of red peppers, strung up to dry in the September sunshine.

Families and workers spend their days out on the land, backs aching after hours spent twisting the fruit from the plants, not stopping until every last one is in a basket in the back of the lorry. On the margins of the field a pot-bellied cauldron simmers over an open fire, full inevitably of a paprika-laden stew to fuel the workers.

The passion for paprika probably has its roots in the turmoil of the 16th century, when the Ottoman Turks invaded Hungary. The Turks passed on their fondness for chillies, which they may have acquired from Italy, or from India, via Persia. In the early days the long, red hot peppers were grown principally for their decorative value, but gradually the peasantry discovered that they grew easily, and brought a zest to dull food.

That's one story, but it may be that the paprika peppers made their way to Hungary through Europe, again grown as ornamentals rather than spice plants. No one knows for sure but it took almost 200 years for them to gain dominion over the Hungarian diet.

There's no rigid rule distinguishing paprika from ground chilli. Both are made from ground dried *Capsicum annum* varieties (a group that also includes bell peppers). The biggest difference is heat, but even here there is an overlap. Paprika ranges from mild and sweet to hot and lively. The American Spice Trade Association suggests that paprikas should score somewhere between 0 and 500 on the Scoville Heat Scale (explained on page 17); anything more and we are heading into chilli territory. Now I don't want to quibble but I've come across one or two brands of hot paprika that have made my eyes water just as much as an average mild chilli, but these must merely be the exceptions that prove the wishy-washy rule.

Hungary may be the most famous paprika-producing country, but Spain rivals it for quality and originality. Two areas are of particular note: Murcia and La Vera in Extremadura in western Spain. Here the spice is known as pimentón, a variation on the Spanish for pepper. Colombus and his conquistadors, desperate to go home with valuable black pepper, branded New World chillies with the same name because of their searing heat.

For me it's the paprika from La Vera that really stands out. The peppers are not so different from those grown in Murcia, Hungary or the Netherlands, or Africa or Peru, but the drying technique turns the spice into something exceptional. It all started at the Monastery of Yuste, near Cáceres. The monks began to dry their chillies over smouldering oak logs, which gave them a sensational smoky flavour. So began a practice that carries on to this day.

Around the time the monks were honing their smoking pepper techniques, Charles V, Holy Roman Emperor was growing weary of his powerful life, smiting and smoting Protestants and enemies in general. In 1556 he handed over the crown of the Holy Roman Empire to his brother Ferdinand and withdrew from public life to finish his days in that same Monastery of Yuste. Here he spent his last years, with clocks ticking all around him, eating, I hope, food liberally spiced with pimentón, until he succumbed to a fatal bout of malaria a year and a half later.

Perhaps he should have made even more of that smoky seasoning, for it has since been discovered that peppers are miraculously high in Vitamin C, containing three times as much as oranges or lemons. Amongst other things, that makes them rather good for gout, which poor Charles V suffered from terribly, until the malaria got him.

Types of paprika

Paprika falls into one of three groups: Hungarian, Spanish and 'the rest'. Paprika is grown and produced all over the world in increasing quantities. It's quite likely that the tub of paprika you buy at the supermarket may have come from Peru, or Zambia, or a dozen other countries. However, the various Hungarian and Spanish options have distinct characteristics that are worth knowing. ➦

patatas a la extremeña

Serves 4, or 6 as a side dish

3 tablespoons extra virgin olive oil

250g chorizo sausage, skinned and
  roughly sliced

1.5kg large potatoes, peeled and cut into
  3cm chunks

1 red pepper, cored, deseeded and cut
  into long strips

1 green pepper, cored, deseeded and cut
  into long strips

3 garlic cloves, peeled and finely chopped

1 tablespoon smoked pimentón (sweet
  or hot as you wish)

1 bay leaf

salt and freshly ground black pepper

Potatoes love paprika and never more so than in this stew of potatoes, fresh peppers and oodles of smoky pimentón. This version comes from the Extremadura region of Spain, the home of smoked paprika. It also contains a seasoning of chorizo. Look for the softer, semi-dried sausage, designed for cooking rather than eating thinly sliced. Serve it as a side dish or a main dish.

Heat the olive oil in a wide heavy frying pan over a moderate heat. Add the chorizo and fry briskly until lightly browned. It will break up in the process, but that's fine.

Reduce the heat and add all the remaining ingredients. Stir around for a couple of minutes, then pour in just enough water to cover. Bring up to the boil and simmer nice and gently, stirring occasionally, for some 20–30 minutes until the potatoes are cooked and the liquid has reduced by about half. Taste and adjust the seasoning.

Serve with plenty of good bread to mop up the juices.

sea bass with lemon & paprika butter

Serves 2

2 sea bass, about 300g each, descaled
and gutted

½ large lemon (cut vertically, from stalk
end to base)

50g butter, melted

salt and freshly ground black pepper

1 tablespoon sweet paprika

a little chopped parsley

To serve:

lemon wedges

This is a dish with streamlined drama built into it. It's quick to put together, looks stylish with the lemon slices and the startling red butter, and it tastes divine. For a weekday supper, replace the sea bass with whole rainbow trout. Use sweet mild or smoked mild, or even one of the hotter paprikas if you want to add a bit of oomph.

Preheat the oven to 220°C/Gas mark 7. Lay the fish on a board. Slice the lemon half very thinly, discarding the ends — you should be able to cut 12 slices from it. Make 3 slashes across each side of each fish, pushing the blade in at a shallow angle to the bone (not straight down vertically). Tuck a slice of lemon into each cut.

Lay the fish in a buttered baking dish, brush with a little of the melted butter, then season with salt and pepper. Roast the fish for 20 minutes, until just cooked through.

When the fish are just cooked, reheat the melted butter in a small pan until it sizzles, then add the paprika. Spoon some of the paprika butter over the fish and pour the rest into a small jug.

Sprinkle the fish with chopped parsley. Serve immediately, with lemon wedges on the side, handing the remaining paprika butter around.

Hungarian paprika

Genuine Hungarian paprika is probably the best in the world, because it is grown and processed with such devotion. It comes in eight different grades. You're unlikely to come across many of these outside Hungary, but if you do you will know what you are buying:

Special quality *(különleges)* The mildest of all paprikas with a marvellously vibrant red colour

Delicate *(csípösmentes csemege)* Mild, with a full rounded flavour

Exquisite delicate *(csemege paprika)* Like delicate, but with a hint of hot prickle

Pungent exquisite delicate *(csípös csemege)* And another notch up the heat ladder

Noble sweet *(édesnemes)* The most widely used paprika, with a noticeable lick of heat and a bright red colour

Half-sweet *(félédes)* Like noble sweet but with more of a kick to it

Rose *(rózsa)* Subtler red colour, mildly hot

Hot *(erös)* A genuinely hot paprika, light brown-orange in colour

Spanish paprika

The Spanish love paprika too, but they're not quite so obsessive about it as the Hungarians. That means a mere three main sorts of pimentón, with a brace of bolt-ons to keep consumers on their toes:

Sweet *(dulce)* Mild paprika, orange in colour

Medium hot *(agridulce)* Halfway between dulce and picante

Hot *(picante)* The loudest, most pungent paprika

In addition it may be smoked *(ahumado)*. In this case it probably comes from La Vera, which has earned itself a Denominación de Origen, a guarantee of origin and quality. So too has the pimentón from Murcia. ◆◆

smoky chicken kebabs

Serves 4

8 chicken thighs, skinned and boned

Marinade:

2 garlic cloves, peeled

leaves from 1 large tarragon sprig

1 red chilli, deseeded and chopped

coarse salt and freshly ground black
pepper

2 teaspoons mild smoked pimentòn

½ tablespoon tomato purée

2 tablespoons sherry vinegar or red wine
vinegar

4 tablespoons extra virgin olive oil

To serve:

lemon or lime wedges

Never mind the weather, with La Vera pimentón you can get the smoky barbecue effect any time of year. These chicken kebabs, marinated in brick red goo, bring a taste of the barbecue to the table even when you've cooked them under the kitchen grill on a drizzly grey day.

Eat them just as they are, with salads, or slide the sizzling chicken into a pitta pocket and add slices of cucumber and tomato, and strands of watercress.

To prepare the marinade, pound the garlic, tarragon leaves and chilli with a couple of big pinches of salt, to a rough paste in a mortar. Now work in the pimentòn, tomato purée, vinegar, olive oil, a little extra salt, and some pepper.

Cut the chicken into 3cm pieces and place in a dish. Pour on the marinade and turn to coat each piece. Leave for at least half an hour, preferably a lot longer – up to 24 hours – covered, in the fridge.

Preheat the grill or barbecue thoroughly. Thread the chicken pieces onto 8 skewers, then grill or barbecue for 9–10 minutes, turning once, until the chicken is browned and cooked through. Serve immediately.

Buying paprika

Buy paprika in a glass jar so that you can at least see that the colour is bright. A dull, tired hue suggests that the spice has been hanging around for far too long and will taste of nothing. And always buy from a reputable source, particularly when abroad. Unscrupulous producers have been known to dye dusty old paprika to give it an alluring brilliant red colour. And let's not even go into adulteration.

Notes on paprika

✪ To get the best out of paprika, firstly be generous, particularly with the mild ones. This is just a dried red pepper, not a powerful tropical spice, so think in terms of tablespoons, not teaspoons.

✪ Secondly, the full flavour is released by heat, so although it may look pretty sprinkled over scrambled eggs, it won't taste of much. Unfortunately, the relatively high sugar content of paprika means that it burns easily. The trick is to add it to hot fat once you've softened the onions and garlic, or whatever else forms the basis of your dish. Pull the pan off the heat, sprinkle in the paprika and stir well, then add the liquid and simmer everything together.

Cooking with paprika

Paprika works best when it is cooked, so although it can add a jolly splash of red to cold dishes, it won't work any significant magic on their taste. Where it does shine is in almost anything that begins with a pan of fried onions, particularly soups and stews. The classic Hungarian trio – goulash, pörkölt and paprikàs – are, when made well with good ingredients and lashings of paprika, genuinely great creations. And there are plenty more Hungarian paprika dishes where they came from.

Naturally Spain has also spawned some marvellous dishes red with paprika, or rather pimentón. Top in my book would be chilindron – with tomatoes and fresh red peppers as well as pimentón – or a Basque chickpea and chorizo stew chock full of chickpeas in a red lake of sauce.

In fact, paprika goes well with pulses of all kinds, as well as meat or white-fleshed fish. It's used in many seafood recipes in Portugal, whilst over in Turkey it comes into play with vegetables too. Believe it or not, they even make a sweet paprika tart in Kalocsa.

pork pörkölt/pork paprikás

Serves 6

1kg boned shoulder or leg of pork,
  trimmed of excess fat

60g lard or bacon fat

1 large onion, peeled and chopped

2 tablespoons sweet paprika

1 tablespoon hot paprika

200g tinned chopped tomatoes (½ tin)

salt and freshly ground black pepper

300ml water

150g crème fraîche (optional)

Here we have two great Hungarian dishes in one recipe. The first is the pörkölt, a brick-red stew, rich and seductive. Add soured cream to a pörkölt and you have paprikàs. Together they showcase the whole point of paprika. Used in considerable quantity – both sweet and hot – it comes to life, with its wonderful rounded, caramelised pepper taste.

For the pork paprikás, I deviate from the genuine recipe by using crème fraîche (the full-fat version, which doesn't split when heated). If you prefer to use soured cream, stir it into the stew off the heat just before serving.

Either way, serve pörkölt/paprikás with buttered noodles, or simple boiled potatoes.

Cut the pork into roughly 3cm cubes. Heat half the lard or bacon fat in a flameproof casserole or heavy-based saucepan. Add the onion and fry gently until softened, then scoop out and reserve. Add the remaining fat to the casserole and turn the heat up to high. Brown the pork in the fat in two batches.

Once the second batch is browned, take the pan off the heat, wait 20–30 seconds, then stir in both paprikas. Quickly return the first batch of meat to the pan with the onion and stir until nicely mixed.

Add the tomatoes, some salt and pepper, and the water. Bring up to the boil, then turn the heat right down low. Cover and simmer very gently for 1 hour, stirring occasionally, until the pork is tender. Skim off as much fat as you can.

Stir in the crème fraîche, if using. Taste and adjust the seasoning, then serve.

What connects lyophilisation, garbling, Yale University and witches? Given the chapter heading, the answer is obvious, but it is the how that's interesting. Let's begin at the beginning. Pepper is native to the Malabar Coast of southern India. It is a glossy-leaved climbing vine that will scale heights of up to 10 metres, given the chance. Cultivated pepper is usually pruned back to a mere 3.5–4 metres, and is supported by either a support tree, or a wooden pole or struts. Each vine produces 20–30 stems of tightly hugging white or pink flowers, which take 6–8 months to turn into fully ripened peppercorns.

pepper

For millennia pepper has been coveted and traded at considerable cost to human life, as well as financially. Long before the Europeans finally found their way to Malabar and Sumatra, Arab traders were transporting this precious cargo across the oceans. Everyone wanted a taste of this new wonder. Even Alaric, king of the Visigoths, lusted after pepper and demanded a ransom of 3,000 lbs of peppercorns during his siege of Rome.

Having set this bellicose attitude, others followed in his wake. No wonder that the Portuguese, then the Dutch East India Company began slaughtering their way to pepper wealth, followed by the British East India Company and others. These were nasty, brutish times, the misery and murder justified by the promise of a ship's hold, or even a pocketful of peppercorns.

Elihu Yale worked for the British East India Company and in 1687 was made Governor of Fort Saint George in Madras, now Chennai. He had spent the first few years of his life in Boston, Massachusetts. He was a wheeler-dealer, running underhand operations under the as-yet-non-existent radar, and he made himself a massive fortune. One of his most successful spots of moonlighting began with the dispatching of a brace of his henchmen across the Bay of Bengal to Aceh in Sumatra to negotiate a new and exclusive pepper trade. It took several generations for the trade to get established, but eventually American ships were carrying it across the oceans to Salem. It was this trade that transformed the small town into a major trading port. To this day, the Seal of the City of Salem carries a picture of a native Achenese and the motto, 'To the farthest port of the rich east'.

Around the same time as Elihu was opening up the pepper trade to the world in the early 1690s, the sorry tale of the Salem Witches was unfolding. The heyday of Salem's spice trade came 100 years later in the 18th and early 19th centuries, drawing to a close in 1846.

Elihu Yale, meanwhile, returned to England and dabbled in the diamond trade. He received a request for support from the Collegiate School in New Haven, Connecticut. He obliged royally, and they renamed the school Yale College, later Yale University, after him. The foundations of this world-famous educational institution are built on finest Sumatran black pepper.

While pepper is no longer the stuff of fabulous fortune, it is still a hugely important commodity and the most widely traded spice in the world. The biggest producer today is Vietnam (25%), followed by Indonesia, then India, down in third place now, and Brazil. Black, white, green and red peppercorns all come from the same plant. The differences depend on harvesting and finishing techniques, some ancient, others quite modern.

Once peppercorns – white or black – are dried, they are then garbled. Well, the classy ones are, anyway. On spice merchants' websites the highest prices are charged for MG1 or TGEB, or if you are after the very best, TGSEB. The initials stand for Malabar Garbled 1, Tellicherry Garbled Extra Bold, and Tellicherry Garbled Special Extra Bold. In this context 'garbled' simply means sorted, cleansed of all debris and sieved to get uniformly sized peppercorns. 'Bold' refers to size: the bolder the bigger and better. Malabar and Tellicherry refer to the quality of the peppercorns, rather than the exact place they are grown, Tellicherry being India's finest.

For centuries the only options were black or white peppercorns, then in the 1970s along came lyophilisation and green peppercorns were born. Lyophilisation is the technical term for freeze-drying. This is not, as I had imagined, a 20th century invention. The ancient Incas, high up in the cool and often icy Andes got there first. They discovered that if you left potatoes out overnight, and then stomped on the frozen tubers to expel every last drop of moisture, they would keep, either whole or ground to a powder (surely the very first instance of instant mash). These freeze-dried potatoes were known as chuño. Although modern freeze-drying is more sophisticated, the principle remains the same. ➥

amalfi's peppered mussels

Serves 4

2kg fresh mussels

3 tablespoons extra virgin olive oil

3 garlic cloves, peeled and chopped

150ml white wine

½–1 teaspoon coarsely ground black
  pepper

salt

juice of 1 lemon

1 tablespoon chopped parsley

This excellent dish of sweet orange mussels seasoned with oodles of black pepper comes from Italy's Amalfi Coast. Use a pestle and mortar to crush the pepper, or pulse in an electric grinder taking care to keep it coarse.

Serve the '*mpepate di cozze* with finger bowls and napkins for sticky fingers, soup spoons for the juices, and warm ciabatta for mopping the plate.

Clean the mussels thoroughly: begin by tipping them gently into the sink, then turning on the cold tap. One by one, scrub each mussel, scraping away any barnacles and tugging off the wiry beard. Tap any open mussels firmly, and if they stay open throw them out. Discard any mussels with broken shells too. Rinse out the sink, then return the mussels to it and cover with cold water. Swish them around gently, then let them stand for a few minutes so that any grit falls to the bottom. Scoop out the mussels into a colander and set aside.

Heat the olive oil gently in a big saucepan or flameproof casserole and add the garlic. Let it cook quietly for a minute or so until golden brown. Swiftly pour in the wine at arm's length (the hot oil will spit and sizzle), then tip in the mussels. Clamp on the lid, turn up the heat, and steam the mussels, shaking the pan from time to time, until they have opened; this should take no longer than 5 minutes. Discard any that stay stubbornly shut.

Scoop the mussels out into a serving bowl; keep warm. Filter the cooking juices (through a sieve lined with a coffee filter paper or muslin) into a small pan to remove any grit, and then warm through. Stir in the pepper and taste to see if salt is needed; it probably won't be.

Pour the peppery juices over the mussels. Squeeze the lemon juice on top and sprinkle with chopped parsley. Serve at once.

prawn, mango & avocado salad

Serves 4

16–20 shelled large raw prawns

1 ripe mango

1 ripe avocado

60g small salad leaves

juice of 2 limes

salt

3 tablespoons sunflower oil

1 tablespoon drained red peppercorns
  in brine

small handful of coriander, roughly
  chopped

To serve:

1 lime, cut into wedges

The strange, aromatic heat of soft, ripe red peppercorns gives a vivid edge to one of my favourite combinations: prawn, mango and avocado with lots of lime juice. If you can't get red peppercorns, try it with brined or fresh green ones instead.

If they are damp, pat the prawns dry on kitchen paper. Peel, halve, stone and slice the mango and avocado thinly. Mix the sliced fruit with the salad leaves and divide between 4 plates. Squeeze over the juice of one of the limes and season with salt.

Heat the oil in a large frying pan. Add the prawns and fry for 4 minutes or so, turning once, until they have turned a good-humoured pink. Scatter over the peppercorns and shake the pan for a few seconds to heat them through. Now take the pan off the heat, squeeze over the juice of the other lime and season with salt.

Spoon the prawns, peppercorns and pan juices over the salads. Scatter over the coriander and serve swiftly, with lime wedges.

pot-roast guinea fowl with green peppercorns

Serves 3

60g butter

1 tablespoon sunflower oil

1 guinea fowl, 1.1–1.2kg

500g pearl onions, skinned

1 heaped tablespoon green peppercorns
  in brine, with their juice

1½ tablespoons brandy

1½ tablespoons Benedictine, if you have
  it, or another 1½ tablespoons brandy

about 250ml chicken stock

salt

While on holiday in France, my mother cut this recipe – originally for duck – from the local paper. She made it with less fatty guinea fowl and it swiftly became a firm family favourite.

Skinning the little onions can be tedious, but if you top, tail and cover them with boiling water for a minute or so, the skins should slip off easily once you drain them.

Heat the butter and oil in a large frying pan and brown the guinea fowl and onions, turning to colour all over.

Transfer the guinea fowl and onions to a deep, flameproof casserole and add the green peppercorns, alcohol and 4 tablespoons of stock. Sprinkle a little salt over the onions.

Cover tightly and cook gently until the bird is done, about 45–60 minutes, turning it over occasionally and basting it with a little more stock, but keep the liquid level low. To check, pierce the thickest part of the thigh with a skewer – the juices should run clear, not pink.

Lift out and carve the bird, arranging it on a hot, shallow serving dish with the onions. Season with salt. Skim the fat from the pan juices, taste and adjust the seasoning. Add a little more stock, but only enough to lighten; the sauce should not be copious. Pour over the bird and serve.

Freeze-drying was a gift to pepper farmers, allowing them to harvest some of their crop early. It has come into play again more recently with the introduction of the first truly ripe, red peppercorns with their evocative, fruity pepper scent. They are still hard to come by, but good delis and mail-order spice companies will stock them.

And that explains how the small, wrinkled, black orbs that lurk unappreciated in your peppermill link together lyophilisation, garbling, Yale University and witches.

Types of pepper

Green peppercorns Picked when the pepper berries have swelled to their full size but are still way off ripeness, these are the babies. They are already pungent, but have a wonderful, slightly floral, slightly metallic taste. Being young, they are comparatively tender. You can buy them freeze-dried (good for a peppermill) or in brine or vinegar, better for recipes where they are used whole. Best of all are the fresh or frozen ones available from good Asian food stores.

Black peppercorns These are picked green just as one or two berries of a bunch are beginning to turn red. In many pepper-growing areas they are blanched for a few minutes in boiling water, then dried, to speed up drying. On drying, the outer skin darkens and wrinkles.

White peppercorns Left on the plant to mature for longer, these are just-ripened peppercorns. Once picked, they are sealed in jute bags, then retted, or as one Indian producer preferred to say, water-roasted. In other words, the bags are submerged in running water for several days, until the soft skins are washed away. The naked peppercorns have gathered a little extra flavour through staying on the vine longer than black ones, but much of that is lost with the skin, leaving just a hot white spice.

Red peppercorns The latest addition to the clan, these are allowed to ripen fully. They have a beautiful fruitiness and a touch of sweetness but they still pack a mighty punch. Buy them freeze-dried and they'll be more of a rusty brown, or bottled in brine which preserves their rosy hue.

Pink peppercorns These are not peppercorns at all. They come from a shrub called *Schinus molle*, native to Peru. Their sole merit is prettiness, as their flavour is none too pleasant, but, contrary to common belief they are not toxic. ☛

chinese caramelised salt & pepper walnuts

Serves 6

120g shelled walnut pieces

170g caster or granulated sugar

60ml water

1 level teaspoon coarse salt, crushed

1 level teaspoon freshly crushed black
   pepper

Every time I make this, guests' initial scepticism disappears as speedily as the sweet, salt and hot nuts themselves. This is, I suppose, the Chinese answer to Louisiana's pralines. But with pepper.

Preheat the oven to 200°C/Gas mark 6. Spread the walnuts out on a baking tray and roast for 3–4 minutes. Tip them into a metal sieve and shake over a sheet of paper to get rid of as much loose skin as possible.

Put the sugar and water into a heavy-based pan and stir over a medium heat until the sugar is completely dissolved. Now stop stirring and boil the syrup, swirling the pan occasionally, to even out hotspots, until it reaches the soft-ball stage; i.e. when a little of the sugar syrup dropped into a glass of iced water forms a soft but not sticky ball. As soon as you are there, tip the walnuts, salt and pepper into the sugar syrup.

Stir and keep on boiling until the syrup reaches the hard-ball stage; i.e. when a drop of syrup in a glass of iced water forms a hard ball. Immediately tip the mixture out onto a greased baking tray and spread out as best you can, pulling apart the walnuts with a fork.

Leave to cool before eating.

Szechuan pepper A terrific, under-used and under-rated spice. It is not related to pepper, and its considerable heat is rather different in nature. Szechuan pepper tingles on the tongue in a unique way, and carries a citrus note in its wake. It is much used, not only in Szechuan but also in Japan, where it provides the essential heat in Japanese seven-spice blend (see page 211). To release the full force of Szechuan pepper, it is essential to dry-fry it.

Long pepper This is related to black pepper, but the small berries clustered on flowering spikes fuse together as they grow to form a cone, about 3cm long. It is hotter than ordinary pepper, with a warm, sweetish almost earthy flavour.

Cubeb pepper This member of the black pepper family is native to Indonesia. The corns are slightly larger than those of true pepper, and as well as the usual heat, have a bitter under-taste.

Mignonette pepper Usually a blend of coarsely cracked black and white pepper. Used in classic French dishes. Also called shot pepper.

Cooking with pepper

Since almost every savoury dish in the world contains pepper, you already know plenty about how to use this spice, but let me put in a plea first of all for generosity. A couple of snappy twists of a peppermill over the pan isn't enough. Make it 5 or 6, or even 10 twists if you want to get pepper doing its job of enlivening what you eat. And, if you happen to have any, jettison those tubs of ready-ground grey dust that lose all their animation in a matter of weeks.

Domestic cooks can live without white pepper. On the whole, it's reserved for spicing up dishes such as béchamel or mashed potatoes, where chefs want to avoid specks of black. Unless this is a problem for you, I can't see what harm the odd black dot does in with spuds, and you get all that gorgeous aroma that is lacking in white pepper.

Don't forget that pepper is a proper spice, as well as a pedestrian touch of seasoning. Dare to give it more prominence occasionally, and not only on a steak. Pepper can be every bit as thrilling as chilli.

Green and red peppercorns, preserved in brine or fresh, are soft enough to be squished between your fingers, though generally they are used whole – in sauces, stir-fries and pâtés for instance. Freeze-dried green peppercorns need to be ground either in a mortar or peppermill to release their prowess; you can also rehydrate them in a little warm water to restore something of their original state.

peppernotter

Makes about 75

270g plain flour

75g cornflour

1 teaspoon baking powder

¼ teaspoon salt

½ level teaspoon freshly ground black
   pepper

½ level teaspoon ground cardamom

½ teaspoon ground cinnamon

¼ teaspoon ground cloves

225g butter, softened

¼ teaspoon vanilla extract

225g caster sugar

4 tablespoons double cream

85g blanched almonds, finely chopped

Peppernotter (literally 'peppernuts') are a Christmas treat right across Scandinavia and down into Germany where they become *pfeffernüsse*. There are many different variations of these spiced biscuits, but most treat pepper as a spice like any other, a lingering habit that has been handed down since medieval times. In this version pepper is blended with cardamom, cinnamon, cloves and vanilla to invigorate these little crumbly biscuits.

Preheat the oven to 180°C/Gas mark 4. Sift the flour with the cornflour, baking powder, salt and ground spices. In a large bowl, cream the butter with the vanilla extract. Add the sugar and beat until light and fluffy.

Gradually work in the flour mixture, a few spoonfuls at a time, alternating with single spoonfuls of cream. Finally, stir in the chopped almonds.

Roll the dough into little balls, about 2cm in diameter, and place them on ungreased baking sheets, spacing about 2.5cm apart. Bake for about 15 minutes until golden. Leave on the baking sheets for a minute or two to firm up slightly, then transfer to wire racks to cool.

Store in an airtight tin for up to a week.

fenugreek

sumac

turmeric

bitter & sour spices

On the evening of 27th October 2005, New Yorkers out for an evening stroll noticed something strange but not entirely unappealing. The sweet scent of maple syrup hung over the city. It happened again 6 months later in March 2006. And again in November that year. For three and a half years the mystery lingered. Some shrugged their shoulders, others worried about airborne toxins, or worse, chemical warfare.

fenugreek

It wasn't until the morning of 5th February 2009 that the truth of the matter emerged. Mayor Bloomberg called a press conference at County Hall. The culprit, they had finally discovered, was International Frutarom Corporation, a few miles to the west in New Jersey. Their crime nothing more serious than the processing of fenugreek, to extract an essence destined to flavour artificial maple syrup. Come to think of it, fake maple syrup is a crime, but of a different order.

Until I read about this incident I'd never thought much about the scent of fenugreek seeds. They're so hard and stony that you assume there is precious little smell. How wrong can you be? When I opened a fresh packet of fenugreek seeds, I was instantly struck by a powerful curry smell, but where was the maple syrup? To find it you need to rub the seeds together firmly, then take a big sniff. You will swiftly detect a sweet maple scent that seems at odds with their dominant bitter flavour. You're even more likely to notice it on a hot day if you stand next to someone who has consumed a lot of fenugreek. The whiff of maple syrup sweat and maple syrup breath is a dead give-away.

But why would anyone consume large amounts of fenugreek? As with so many spices fenugreek is a bit of a wunderkind, with a reputation for curing, or at least alleviating a variety of ailments from the trivial (flatulence and baldness) to the serious (diabetes). For centuries, fenugreek seeds have been taken to increase the milk flow of nursing mothers, often with astonishing speed and effectiveness, and apparently with no side effects, other than a gentle sweet aura. Actually, it doesn't take much fenugreek to get that aura, as I've just discovered. After two nights of fenugreek-laced suppers, the tips of my fingers are oddly, sweetly fragrant.

In fact, fenugreek is an all-round crowd-pleaser. It grows with considerable ease and speed, is not too temperamental and virtually every part of it, bar the root, can be eaten. It has been grown for millennia, particularly in North Africa, and takes its name from the ancient Greek practice of feeding dried fenugreek plants to domestic animals. *Foenum* means hay and *graecum* means of Greece.

It has been taken in throughout India, where the plant is known as *methi*. The green leaves are used both as herb and vegetable (a slightly bitter spinach), often cooked with potatoes or other starchy ingredients. The seeds are, of course, used in curries, and as a medicine and in cosmetics. That's just the start. Soaked seeds become soft and mucilaginous, and are excellent in salads and other dishes. What's more you can sprout them as they do in India, then eat them raw or cook them with other spices.

Fenugreek seeds are odd little things, a tawny pale brown, very angular, shaped like a skewed rectangle, and so, so hard. They grow, twenty or more at a time, side by side in a long beaky pod, which points suggestively upward. Not surprisingly, this has led to a hopeful belief that fenugreek will cure impotence. There seems to be little evidence to support this.

Notes on fenugreek

✿ There is really no point in buying ground fenugreek as it is unlikely that you will be using it in any great quantity. It's much wiser to invest in a bigger packet of whole fenugreek seeds from an Asian or Middle Eastern food shop. For a start they will keep for months, and secondly you can use them both as spice and grain.

✿ Grinding whole fenugreek seeds is not the easiest of tasks, but a few minutes of serious pounding in a good mortar will do the trick. Dry-fried, they are crisp and easy to pulverise.

✿ If you want to taste the soft side of fenugreek, soak the seeds in plenty of cold water for 5–6 hours or longer, until they are tender. Drain and use them raw. ➥

newari fenugreek & tomato salad

Serves 4

50g fenugreek seeds

2 tablespoons sunflower oil

3 garlic cloves, peeled and chopped

1cm piece fresh root ginger, chopped

2 green jalapeño or Fresno chillies,
    quartered lengthways and deseeded

1 teaspoon cumin seeds

½ teaspoon ground turmeric

1 onion, peeled and chopped

4 tomatoes, deseeded and chopped

2 tablespoons toasted sesame seeds

juice of 1 lime

salt and freshly ground black pepper

Methi ko achar is something of a favourite in the foothills of Kathmandu. The soaked fenugreek loses most of its bitterness, adding instead a mild softness that reminds me of the taste of immature wheat grains, the ones that you chew from a head of wheat on an early summer walk.

Be sure to add the cooked vegetables to the bowl of fenugreek. If you tip the fenugreek into the hot pan, as I did the first time, some of the seeds will harden in the drying heat.

Put the fenugreek seeds into a small bowl, add cold water to cover and leave to soak for 3 hours.

Drain the fenugreek seeds and tip into a saucepan. Cover with fresh cold water and bring to a simmer over a medium heat. Simmer for 10 minutes until tender. Drain and rinse under the cold tap, then transfer to a serving bowl.

Heat the oil in a wide frying pan over a medium heat and add the garlic, ginger and chillies. Fry, stirring, until beginning to colour. Add the cumin seeds and turmeric and fry for a further 30 seconds.

Add the onion and fry, stirring, for 2–3 minutes. Now add the chopped tomatoes and toss for a few seconds to soak up the spices. Tip the contents of the frying pan onto the fenugreek seeds and add the sesame seeds and lime juice. Season with salt and pepper to taste and serve.

griddled black-spiced beef with sumac yoghurt

Serves 3–4

600–700g rump or sirloin steak, 4–5cm thick, in one or two pieces

salt

Spice rub:

½ teaspoon fenugreek seeds

1 teaspoon cumin seeds

1 teaspoon coriander seeds

½ teaspoon fennel seeds

¼ teaspoon cayenne pepper

4 tablespoons extra virgin olive oil

To serve:

3 heaped tablespoons thick Greek yoghurt

2 teaspoons sumac

6 Cos lettuce leaves, thickly shredded

I'm determined now to use more fenugreek in my cooking, not just in curries, but in simpler, more immediate dishes like this one. A punchy spice rub – with ample doses of fenugreek, coriander and cumin – gives an extra-thick, extra-juicy steak a gorgeous piquancy. Splash out on a well-hung rump or sirloin steak, with a good marbling of fat, and ask your butcher to cut it thickly.

First make the spice rub. Dry-fry the whole spices in a frying pan until they give off a seductive aroma, and the fenugreek is a shade or two darker. Cool slightly, then crush to a powder using a spice grinder or pestle and mortar. Mix the crushed spices with the cayenne and olive oil.

Smear the spice rub over both sides of the steak(s), then cover loosely and leave to marinate for 2–6 hours, in the fridge.

Preheat the oven to 220°C/Gas mark 7. Mix the yoghurt with the sumac. Heat an oiled ovenproof griddle pan over a high heat until blisteringly hot. Lay the steak(s) on the griddle pan and cook for 2 minutes on each side. Turn again quickly, transfer to the oven and cook for a further 5–7 minutes.

Transfer the steak to a board and let it rest in a warm spot for 4–5 minutes. Divide the shredded lettuce between 4 plates, or spread over a single large serving plate.

Season the hot steak with salt, slice it thinly and arrange on top of the lettuce. Serve straight away, with the sumac-flavoured yoghurt.

Cooking with fenugreek

Fenugreek is a spice that marries a host of contradicting scents and flavours, making it that much more demanding to incorporate in everyday cooking. For most of us, the primary use of fenugreek will always be as an important constituent in curry powders and spice mixes, to which it brings a full, balancing bitter note that rounds out other spices. In cheaper commercial curry powders it may be used to bulk out other more expensive spices, bringing its wonderful curry smell, but overwhelming all else. Better, as always, to mix up your own spices as you need them, adding a moderate dose of fenugreek.

In the north of India, the Newari tribe of Nepal are keen aficionados of fenugreek seeds. They like them soft and plentiful, soaking and sprouting the seeds to use in salads and rice dishes galore. In Bengal, fenugreek is one of the five spices used in panch phoron (see page 213). Elsewhere it is the green leaf that is preferred, thrown by the handful into the pan to flavour wonderful meals of fragrant chicken, fish or vegetables.

The most surprising fenugreek dishes, however, are made in Africa, particularly in the Yemen, Ethiopia and Eritrea. Here fenugreek has become a staple, soaked and swollen and beaten to a paste. Does this still count as a spice? Probably not... but there aren't many spices that can multi-task with such ease. Fenugreek is also an essential ingredient in the fiercely hot spice paste berbere, which brings many Ethiopian slow-cooked stews to vibrant life.

To sprout fenugreek seeds

Put 2–3 tablespoons fenugreek seeds in a fairly large glass jar and pour in enough cold water to cover. Cover the jar with a square of muslin and secure tightly with an elastic band. Leave at room temperature overnight or for 6–8 hours.

Next day, tip the jar carefully over the sink to drain off the water through the muslin. Once again, pour in fresh cold water to just cover, shake gently to rinse the seeds, then drain out all the water.

Leave somewhere out of direct sunlight, but at room temperature; they don't have to go into a dark cupboard. Carefully rinse and drain the seeds twice a day for 3–4 days until the sprouts have popped up and put on a centimetre or so of growth. Now they are ready to eat, in salads, stir-fries or in a spicy pilau. They are best used straight away, but will keep in an airtight container in the fridge for up to a week, as long as you rinse them every couple of days.

paneer, asparagus & broad bean butter masala

Serves 4

1 teaspoon cumin seeds

1 teaspoon coriander seeds

¼ teaspoon fenugreek seeds

seeds from 5 cardamom pods

½ teaspoon ground turmeric

½ teaspoon cayenne pepper

1–2 tablespoons sunflower oil

225g paneer, cut into 2cm cubes

1 onion, peeled and roughly chopped

3 garlic cloves, peeled and roughly chopped

2cm piece fresh root ginger, peeled and roughly chopped

30g butter

3 tablespoons tomato purée

1 cinnamon stick

1 bay leaf

1 teaspoon caster sugar

salt

200ml water

250g asparagus, trimmed and cut into 3cm lengths

200g podded small broad beans

4 tablespoons natural full-fat yoghurt

2 tablespoons double cream

I make no claims that this is an authentic recipe for paneer butter masala, but I have no hesitation in telling you that it is absolutely gorgeous. I've matched the paneer (Indian cheese, now sold in most good supermarkets) with spring asparagus and broad beans. Magic. Later on in the year, you can replace the spring vegetables with green beans, courgettes or whatever is in season.

Use a natural yoghurt with 4% fat or slightly more – a very low-fat version is likely to curdle – and be sure to whisk it before stirring into the curry, as this helps it to mix in smoothly. Incidentally, if you use frozen broad beans, thaw them first, then stir into the curry with the paneer.

Serve the curry with rice if you wish, but I think it is better scooped up out of the dish with warm chapattis.

Dry-fry the cumin, coriander and fenugreek seeds in a hot, dry pan for about a minute until fragrant. Tip into a bowl and let cool for a few minutes, then add the cardamom seeds and grind to a powder. Stir in the turmeric and cayenne.

Heat the oil in a frying pan, add the paneer and fry, turning, over a brisk heat until coloured on all sides. Remove and drain on kitchen paper; set aside.

In a blender or food processor, blitz the onion, garlic and ginger with 2 tablespoons water to a purée. Heat the butter in a wide frying pan, scrape in the onion purée and fry, stirring constantly, until it starts to colour and you can see oily melted butter seeping out. Stir in the ground spices and cook for another 30 seconds or so.

Now stir in the tomato purée, cinnamon stick, bay leaf, sugar, some salt and the water. Once it starts bubbling, add the asparagus and broad beans. Simmer for 4–5 minutes.

Whisk the yoghurt in a bowl vigorously for a few seconds, then stir it into the sauce 1 tablespoon at a time. Add the paneer to the pan and simmer for a few minutes more, just to heat it through and to finish cooking the asparagus. Taste and adjust the seasoning, adding more salt if needed.

Just before serving, drizzle the cream over the curry in a spiral or any other pattern that grabs your fancy. Serve with chapattis or naan breads.

You may have a sumac bush in your garden. It's a handsome shrub with long leaves arranged in neat serried pairs along each slender branch, and in late summer a candle flame of rust-red, velvet berries pointing skywards. Pause before you rush out to harvest these berries. There are around 250 members of the Rhus family and unless you live in the Middle East or southern Italy, your sumac is unlikely to be *Rhus coriaria*, the tree that has bestowed the tart fruity spice sumac on the lucky people of Sicily, Asia Minor and North Africa.

sumac

One thing many of the sumacs hold in common is a high tannin content, which is reflected in the clean astringent notes of the spice, but more importantly makes them highly useful in the business of tanning leather. Tanning is a stinking, lengthy process, involving endless stages to remove fat, meat and hairs, to destroy bacteria that would rot the skins, and to render them supple, smooth and workable. Sumac's anti-bacterial pyrogallol tannins bond with the protein molecules in the raw skins, tightening the pores and squeezing out moisture.

The stench of the Marrakesh tanneries assaults the nostrils long before you get close. Turn the corner and the sight of dozens of pits awash with evil-looking solutions is startling. For centuries Moroccan leather has been sought after by upholsterers and bookbinders. Usually made of goatskin, it is a pale cream to light brown colour, supple and soft, and very long lasting. It's the bark and leaves that are the source of tanning sumac, sometimes cultivated commercially, often gathered from the wild.

Sumac the spice is a different matter altogether. It remains a little known flavouring outside the eastern and southern Mediterranean and I have no idea why. It may be that it was simply a domestic afterthought, the perk for those who gathered the leaves and bark for the tanneries. The name comes from the ancient Aramaic word for dark red, and you can see why – the best sumac powder is a distinctive deep burgundy purple. It is nothing more nor less than the dried fruit of the sumac, picked when nearly fully ripe, sun-dried and ground to a powder.

American Indians make a refreshing lemonade from sumac. In Iran, sumac takes on a special importance at Norouz (new year), celebrated in the spring. The Haft Sin, the seven S's are gathered on the new year dinner table, each one hugely symbolic. Though the list may vary from family to family, one of the S's is always sumac, the spice of life. Other S's may include garlic (*seer*), vinegar (*serkeh*), red apples (*seeb*), the oleaster fruit (*senjed*), wheat grass (*sabzeh*), coins (*sekeh*), and a hyacinth (*sonbol*).

Notes on sumac

✿ Whole dried sumac berries are a rare commodity outside their home territory, so most of us will have to make do with the ready-ground spice. Sumac varies enormously in colour and intensity depending on provenance. Paler tends to mean milder, so a brick-red powder gives you a light acidity, whilst a dark burgundy purple is far sharper and brighter. This means that when following recipes you need to go by taste rather than adhere strictly to measurements.

✿ Poor-quality stale ground sumac is sometimes adulterated with citric acid to lift the sharpness, but I suspect that this is a bigger issue in sumac countries than elsewhere. As usual, the moral is that you get what you pay for. The bargain bucket sumac snapped up on holiday may not be as good a deal as you imagined.

Cooking with sumac

This spice is good with all manner of things – fish, meat, poultry, vegetables, yoghurt, rice, salads, breads and so on. It's a spice for warm days, when you want food that is full of life and vigour. A sprinkling of sumac gives you just that.

It can be used as a rub or in a marinade for anything destined for the grill or barbecue, or just sprinkled on after cooking. In Turkey it is mixed with thinly sliced onions to partner grilled kebabs (see page 68).

Instead of sprinkling it on meat or fish, stir sumac into rice with a knob of butter and some chopped parsley. Or mix with yoghurt, giving it a rosy glow, adding chopped mint if you like, to create a beautiful relish for seared tuna or swordfish.

Blended with thyme and sesame seeds it makes za'atar (see page 212), which is so good mixed with olive oil to smear over bread. Or stir sumac alone with olive oil to make a dip for warm bread.

lebanese spinach pastries

Makes 14–15

Pastry:

250g plain flour

½ x 7g sachet easy-blend dried yeast

½ teaspoon salt

2 tablespoons extra virgin olive oil

about 150ml water

Filling:

200g spinach leaves

1 onion, peeled and chopped

salt and freshly ground black pepper

1 tablespoon sumac

1 tablespoon extra virgin olive oil

Fatayar al Sabaanikh come in several different guises, but for me this is the best, with the spinach made tart with sumac. The filling is made in a surprising fashion, so that the ingredients are only cooked once, in the oven, giving extra freshness.

To make the pastry, mix the flour, yeast and salt together in a bowl. Make a well in the centre and spoon in the olive oil. Mix it into the flour, then add enough water to make a soft, slightly sticky dough. Turn onto a lightly floured surface and knead vigorously for 10 minutes, dusting with flour as needed, until smooth and plump. Return to the bowl, cover with cling film and leave in a warm place until almost doubled in bulk – about 1 hour.

For the filling, chop the raw spinach, then mix with the onion and 1 tablespoon salt. Knead and squeeze the mixture. Within seconds, water will start oozing out. Keep going for a minute or two, until the spinach has shrunk radically and looks as if it's been cooked. Tip into a fine sieve, squeeze to get rid of as much water as possible, then leave to drain.

Preheat the oven to 220°C/Gas mark 7. Mix the spinach with the sumac, the oil and plenty of pepper. Roll out the dough as thinly as you can on a lightly oiled board (wipe the rolling pin with a little oil, too). Stamp out 8–9 cm circles. Place a generous teaspoonful of the mixture in the centre of each circle. Draw the edges of the pastry up over the filling and bring three equidistant points of the circle together at the top. Pinch the pastry edges together firmly along the three seams, like a tri-cornered hat. Place on a greased baking tray and bake for 20 minutes until golden. Eat warm or cold.

lamb kofte kebabs with sumac & onion relish

Serves 4

Kofte:

500g minced lamb

1 slice stale white bread

4 garlic cloves, peeled and crushed

2 tablespoons chopped parsley

1 heaped teaspoon ras-el-hanout (see
   page 216) or ground cumin

salt and freshly ground black pepper

a little olive oil, for brushing

Onion and sumac relish:

1 onion, peeled and thinly sliced

1 tablespoon sumac

¼ tsp salt

1 tablespoon chopped parsley

Salad:

2 tomatoes, halved then sliced
   (or 12 cherry tomatoes, sliced)

12 radishes, sliced

To serve:

warm Arab flat breads, tortillas or pitta
   bread

I'm not one for eating raw onions, or at least I wasn't until I discovered this divinely simple onion and sumac relish. The sumac and salt has a near miraculous effect, softening the brashness of the onion and bringing a zinging lift to it. It's fabulous with grilled meats of all kinds, but you could also try adding it to salads and sandwiches galore. It's the kind of thing that you'll go back to again and again once you get a taste for it.

For the relish, toss the sliced onion with the sumac and salt and set aside.

For the kofte, put the lamb into a mixing bowl. Tear up the bread and soak in a little water for 5–10 minutes until softened. Squeeze out excess water and add the bread to the meat, together with all the remaining ingredients, except the oil. Knead together thoroughly with your hands until the mixture is evenly blended. Divide into 4 portions.

Rinse your hands, then dampen with cold water. Take a portion of the lamb mixture, roll into a long sausage, then flatten and wrap around a skewer, pressing firmly into place, to recreate the original sausage shape. Repeat with the remaining lamb. Cover with cling film and set aside until needed. Wrap the breads in foil.

Preheat the grill (or barbecue) thoroughly. Brush the kebabs with oil and grill close to the heat (or barbecue) until browned, turning to cook evenly; 8–10 minutes should do it. Slide the foil parcel of bread under the grill too, to heat through.

While the kofte are cooking, mix the chopped parsley into the onions and place in a small serving bowl. Pile the tomato and radishes into another bowl. Place on the table.

To eat, take a warm Arab bread and slide the kofte off its skewer onto the bread. Top with the onion relish and some salad, roll up tightly and take a big bite.

Turmeric is one of the big players in spice-based medicinal research. It has humongous powers, and has long been known to have antiseptic, antifungal, anti-inflammatory, insecticidal, and other impressive properties. Modern medical trials are discovering that it may have a role to play in curing or controlling arthritis, dermatitis, irritable bowel syndrome, cancers and even AIDS. Impressive.

turmeric

It also stains mercilessly. This can be a very good thing. Golden rice looks gorgeous. The orange-yellow robes of Buddhist monks, often died with turmeric, so much cheaper than saffron, are beautiful to behold. A telltale splodge of yellow on my white shirt is not a good thing. Not at all. Nor is the sunny stain on the mixing bowl, or the discoloured patch on the chopping board or the daffodil splatter across the tablecloth.

I was introduced to one of the more curious propensities of turmeric stains some years ago, when a fellow food writer and I had to while away an afternoon in Bangkok. What better, between long flights, than a full-scale Thai massage with herb? Two hours later we felt a million dollars, until my stylish friend noticed his white t-shirt was now inelegantly besmirched with brilliant yellow. 'With herb', it seemed, included a strong dose of turmeric. In the nearest toilet, we washed and rubbed the stains with a bar of soap. To his horror the t-shirt was swiftly transformed. Where once there had been gold, there was now a motley collection of vivid pink splashes.

One of the main components of soap, as I'm sure you know, is sodium hydroxide (or caustic soda), alkaline from top to toe. It seems that curcumin, the principal compound in turmeric and the one responsible for the sunshine yellow, is extremely susceptible to alkalines, blushing pinker and pinker the stronger the base. So if you happen to be dyeing a batch of silk, and you want a total egg-yolk orange, you might add a teensy drop of alkaline sodium hydroxide to the turmeric solution. On the other hand, if it's a sharp clean yellow you're after, then you would introduce something acidic – vinegar, tamarind or lemon juice perhaps.

After extensive research in my kitchen and garden, I can report that the best way to remove turmeric stains is to rinse thoroughly as soon as possible, then wash as per normal with a good dose of biological stain remover. I've tried lemon juice and vinegar and other natural products and the results are dismal. The only two natural products that have more than a passing effect on turmeric are sun or frost. A day on the washing line in direct sizzling sunshine, or an overnight on the line in below zero temperatures will work wonders. Pity these are not available to order.

Turmeric is a member of the ginger family, and like ginger is a rhizome, a swollen underground stem packed with nutrients. Fresh turmeric rhizomes are no bigger than your little finger, and if you snap one open the interior is a near fluorescent, carroty orange. The scent is strangely aromatic, a little bitter, a little mustardy, a little antiseptic. These rhizomes grow in a massive subterranean tangle. Towering above them are the long broad leaves, reminiscent of hostas or lilies, and eventually a stunning composition of yellow flowers and red bracts that would have the chicest florist slavering.

Once harvested, the rhizomes are cleaned, then boiled for an hour or more, which reduces the raw earthy taste and gelatinises the starches, making them easier to dry. This is particularly important when the turmeric is to be sun-dried. The hard, dried rhizomes are tossed in a big tumble drier, to remove scaly scraps of skin. Now they are ready to be sold whole, or ground to the fine yellow powder that imparts an essential flavour to so many curries, and stains so many white shirts.

Notes on turmeric

✪ There are few choices when it comes to buying turmeric. Ground or ground. This means that you are likely to end up with a half-used jar of stale turmeric idling at the back of your cupboard. Be strong enough to throw it out and replace it next time you need turmeric. Wasteful? Possibly, but even if the colour is still good, the aroma will be negligible.

✪ Actually, you can get turmeric in other forms, but you'll probably have to go out of your way to find it. My local Asian food store sells both whole dried chunks of turmeric and fresh juicy rhizomes. ●◆

cashew nut & pea curry

Serves 6

300g cashew nuts, soaked in cold water
   for 2 hours

½ teaspoon ground turmeric

1 lemongrass stem

2 tablespoons sunflower or rapeseed oil

2 onions, peeled, halved and sliced

2 garlic cloves, peeled and chopped

½ cinnamon stick

2 bay leaves

¼ teaspoon cayenne pepper

½ teaspoon mild paprika

1 tablespoon Sri Lankan roasted curry
   powder (see page 214)

300ml coconut milk

salt

150g peas (frozen or fresh)

In Sri Lanka, where this curry comes from, it is made with fresh cashew nuts, which are soft and sweet. Boiling dried cashew nuts gives something of the same nature, while a touch of turmeric gilds them a delicate primrose yellow.

Drain the cashew nuts, then simmer in lightly salted water with the turmeric for about 30 minutes or until soft and creamy-textured. Drain.

Meanwhile, trim the top off the lemongrass stem, leaving just the lower 7–8cm, then crush with the back of a wooden spoon and set aside.

Heat the oil in a saucepan or wok, add the onions and fry for about 5 minutes. Add the garlic, cinnamon and bay leaves and fry for another 3–4 minutes until the onions are tender. Sprinkle over the cayenne, paprika and curry powder and fry for a final 30 seconds or so.

Now pour in the coconut milk and add the lemongrass and some salt. Bring to the boil and add the cashews. Lower the heat and simmer for 5 minutes, then add the peas and simmer for a final 2–3 minutes. Taste and adjust the seasoning, adding a little more salt if needed. Serve at once, with Indian flat breads or chapattis.

golden halibut with spinach dahl

Serves 4

4 pieces halibut fillet, 120–150g each

½ teaspoon ground turmeric

salt

1 tablespoon sunflower oil

Dahl:

200g red lentils

800ml water

1 teaspoon cumin seeds

¼ teaspoon fenugreek seeds

1 teaspoon coriander seeds

45g butter

1 onion, peeled and chopped

2cm piece fresh root ginger, chopped

3 garlic cloves, peeled and chopped

2 red chillies (Fresno or hotter Thai bird chillies), deseeded and cut into fine threads

200g young spinach leaves

2 tomatoes, skinned, deseeded and diced

Both the colour and the strange scent of turmeric transform the simplest fish into something exceptional. Here it sits on a bed of homely red lentil purée – brought to life with a last-minute dose of sizzling spice. As long as your halibut is fresh, there's no need to zip it up with lemon or lime – the spices do the job.

Pat the pieces of fish dry with kitchen paper. Rub with the turmeric and salt, then set aside to absorb the flavours while you make the dahl.

Put the lentils and water into a saucepan and bring to the boil. Lower the heat and simmer gently for 25–30 minutes, stirring occasionally, until the lentils are soft and mushy. Add a little more hot water if you think it is needed, but the final mixture should be fairly thick.

While the lentils are cooking, dry-fry the cumin, fenugreek and coriander seeds in a hot frying pan until fragrant. Tip into a bowl and allow to cool, then grind to a powder.

Melt the butter in the frying pan. When foaming, add the onion, ginger, garlic and chillies and fry until the onion is softened and beginning to brown. Add the ground spices and fry for another minute or so.

Meanwhile, once the lentils are cooked, stir in the spinach a big handful at a time, followed by the tomatoes. Season generously with salt. Tip the hot, sizzling spice mixture into the dahl. Stir, then taste and adjust the seasoning.

To cook the fish, heat the sunflower oil in a large frying pan over a high heat. Fry the halibut quickly, allowing 1–3 minutes on each side, depending on thickness.

To serve, spoon a generous helping of dahl onto each plate and top with a piece of fish. Accompany with rice and sour lime pickles.

The former are so hard that they are near to impossible to grind at home, but fresh rhizomes are worth trying occasionally, especially if you want to delve deeper into the complexities of Thai or Indian culinary tradition. Stored in a sealed plastic bag in the fridge, they will last for a month or more.

✪ Some South-East Asian recipes call for white turmeric, another name for the related spice, zedoary. Real turmeric is not a substitute – better to replace with some severely under-ripe mango, which is closer in taste.

Cooking with turmeric

As far as I can tell, turmeric goes into the majority of all Indian, Pakistani, Bangladeshi and Sri Lankan curries. It is an important spice for three critical reasons. The first is the unique taste, the second is the fabulous colour and the third is its antiseptic quality. It is frequently paired with fish, rubbed in with salt and/or lemon or lime juice before cooking, to ensure that the flesh is pure and safe to eat. Modern refrigeration reduces the importance of this, but colour and flavour are still essential.

Turmeric is often used as the poor man's saffron. It's a cheap colourant, guaranteed to cheer up a pilau or a plain potato dish, but of course, the flavour is totally different. A pinch or two of turmeric amongst the rice and shellfish does not produce a classic paella.

More surprising is the appearance of turmeric in the occasional Middle-Eastern recipe, like the terrific sfouf (see right), one of the few sweet turmeric recipes.

In the UK it has found a special place on the condiment shelf, either blended with mustard powder to give our English mustard its bright yellow colour, or bathing the florets of cauliflower and cubes of carrot in the pickle piccalilli.

If you find some fresh turmeric, try making this Gujerati turmeric pickle: peel and slice the rhizomes, then mix with lime juice. Cover, place in the fridge and ignore for 3 days. Serve with any southern Indian food. Otherwise, slice, chop or grate and use in place of powdered turmeric, in rice dishes, curries and spiced soups.

sfouf

Serves 12

2 tablespoons tahini

300g semolina

250g plain flour

300g caster sugar

1 teaspoon baking powder

½ teaspoon ground turmeric

180g butter, melted and cooled until tepid

300ml milk

1 tablespoon pine nuts

Sfouf… brilliant name, great cake. It comes from the Lebanon, where it is the kind of thing that your granny might bake. A mere half-teaspoon of turmeric gives the crumb a golden glow, as well as a unique mild aroma. Even more unexpected is the tahini, used to grease the baking in. It gives both the base and sides a crispness and subtle sesame scent.

Preheat the oven to 200°C/Gas mark 6. Use the tahini to grease a 25x30cm baking tin, smearing it thickly over the base and sides.

Mix the semolina, flour, sugar, baking powder and turmeric together in a bowl. Make a well in the centre and add the butter and half the milk. Beat well, adding the remaining milk gradually, until evenly combined.

Scrape the mixture into the cake tin and smooth down lightly. Scatter the pine nuts evenly over the surface. Bake for 30–40 minutes, until the sides of the cake are beginning to pull away from the tin and the cake springs back when pressed gently in the middle. Plunge a skewer into the centre – if it comes out clean, then the cake is cooked.

Leave in the tin for 5 minutes, then turn out and finish cooling on a wire rack. Cut into squares or diamonds to serve.

coriander

cumin

juniper

ginger

saffron

aromatic spices

Far, far into a deep dark cave hidden in the hills above the Dead Sea, they stored their precious goods: fabrics, pots, flint tools, painted skulls and rope baskets. They kept stocks of grains and seeds there too: wheat, barley, lentils, pistachio and coriander. Who they were, indeed why they abandoned their hoard of essentials, nobody knows. Archeologists found the remains in 1983, lying in the dust of Nahal Hemel cave, undisturbed for over 8,000 years.

coriander

Another powerful story also places coriander firmly in a Middle Eastern context. In the Bible, when Moses and the Israelites escape the Pharoah and begin their 40-year wander around the Sinai desert, God sends them a miraculous crop of white food, which appears every night, covering the ground like hoarfrost. 'And the house of Israel called the name thereof Manna: and it was like coriander seed, white, and the taste thereof like to flour with honey.' It's a beautiful image, with one teensy snag. Neither coriander seed nor leaf are white. Perhaps it refers to the flowers? Perhaps I'm being too picky? The point is that coriander was familiar not only to those who wrote the Old Testament, but also to the wider community. And not just ordinary people.

In amongst the gold and jewels in Tutankhamun's tomb was a pot of coriander seeds – considered just as important as all the riches for his voyage to the next world.

In North Africa and around the Mediterranean coriander has been part and parcel of the cook's palette for millennia. The Roman cook Apicius used it extensively, both seed and green leaf. The Romans loved it so much that they took it with them wherever they conquered, pillaged and colonised. They even lugged it as far as the British Isles, where it was almost as content to grow as it was in the heat of the Italian sun.

People usually grow coriander for its leaf, but it has an annoying habit of running to seed almost overnight. This offers a rare opportunity to taste a green coriander berry, and even if the crop of coriander leaf is on its last legs, you could still harvest and dry your own spice – a relative rarity outside tropical countries.

The fresh green berry is curious, bridging the massive gap between the flavour of the leaves and the orangey scent of the spice. As the seeds dry, the leafiness fizzles out quietly, leaving the rich citrus note that has made coriander so popular over the centuries. Incidentally, a coriander seed is not technically a seed at all. It's actually two seeds, wrapped up sweetly in a crisp outer layer. And in botanical parlance, that makes it a fruit. So now you know.

Using coriander seed

Coriander is a gentle spice, which never punches above its weight. Used on its own its presence is clear but not aggressive, bringing an orangey, sagey flavour that works a sunny magic with vegetables and pulses. At the top of the coriander dish league are ratatouille and mushrooms à la grecque, both French. Close runner is Elizabeth David's simple salad of sliced raw mushrooms, dressed with a sprinkling of ground coriander, lemon and olive oil.

In the Lebanon coriander is a key ingredient in taklia, a paste stirred into a lentil soup at the end of cooking to give it a vibrant lift. It's easy to make, and a great way to add zest to soups and stews of all kinds: fry 4 sliced garlic cloves in 2 tablespoons clarified butter or olive oil until golden brown. Add 2 teaspoons ground coriander and stir for another 10–20 seconds, then scrape the whole lot into a mortar. Sprinkle over ½ teaspoon coarse salt and pound everything together to form a paste. Try it.

As you would expect, coriander features hugely in many African and Middle Eastern dishes, sometimes on its own but more often with other spices, as in many Moroccan tagines. It reappears in soups, stews, salads and more throughout the Arab world.

It is a natural partner with cumin, but you need to use it in a ratio of at least 2:1, to make sure that it isn't overwhelmed. Dry-fry the two together, then grind finely and you have a spice blend full of Latin American vigour. Try it on a crisp salad of sliced cucumber, radish and watercress, sharpened with a big squeeze of lime juice, and a touch of salt and cayenne. No need for oil. As a double act it reappears in both harissa (see page 19) and dukkah (see page 91).

Coriander is a constituent of numerous curried dishes, playing a major supporting role in spice blends. Because of its mildness, it is frequently the largest component, though barely distinguishable in the finished curry – so often an essential ingredient, but rarely given its due reward. Many drinkers, for instance, would have no idea that coriander is one of the 'botanicals' that flavour gin and a vast number of other spirits and liqueurs.

mushrooms à la grecque

Serves 4

300g button mushrooms

120ml extra virgin olive oil

120ml dry white wine

100ml water

juice of ½ lemon

2 heaped tablespoons tomato purée

1 teaspoon coriander seeds

1 teaspoon black peppercorns

½ teaspoon fennel seeds

1 cinnamon stick

2 generous thyme sprigs

2 bay leaves

salt

Oddly, mushrooms à la Grecque is not particularly Greek, but it is very French. Little pearly button mushrooms are bathed in a delicious pool of gently spiced, slightly sharp, tomatoey juice. It is served at room temperature, usually as part of a mixed hors d'oeuvre. The spices used vary from recipe to recipe, but the one constant is the coriander.

Wipe any dirt off the mushrooms with a damp piece of kitchen paper and set aside.

Put all the remaining ingredients into a saucepan and bring up to the boil. Simmer for 3 minutes, then add the mushrooms. Don't worry if they are not all totally submerged; they'll shrink a little as they cook and all will be well. Simmer for 10 minutes, stirring occasionally. Tip into a bowl and leave to cool.

Serve at room temperature.

lamb dopiaza

Serves 6

900g boned shoulder of lamb

5 large onions

6 tablespoons sunflower or rapeseed oil

8 cardamom pods

8 cloves

6 garlic cloves, peeled and roughly
chopped

3cm piece fresh root ginger, peeled and
roughly chopped

460ml water

½ teaspoon ground cinnamon

½ tablespoon ground cumin

1 tablespoon ground coriander

½ teaspoon cayenne pepper

½ teaspoon ground turmeric

1 teaspoon garam masala (see page 217)

7 tablespoons plain yoghurt

salt

Dopiaza literally means two helpings of onions and that's exactly what you get in this curry, the first batch sliced and fried, and the second puréed with garlic and ginger. And then, of course, there's a blissful array of spices, including plenty of coriander. This is a pretty mild version, but if you want more heat, use 1 teaspoon of cayenne.

Cut the lamb into large chunks and set aside. Chop one of the onions; halve and slice the rest. Heat 5 tablespoons oil in a wide, deep casserole or saucepan and fry the sliced onions until very tender and browned at the edges. Scoop out onto kitchen paper to drain.

Now return the pan to a medium-high heat and add half the lamb with 4 cardamom pods and 4 cloves. Brown the meat all over, then take it out of the pan and set aside. Brown the second batch of meat with the remaining whole spices in the same way.

In the meantime, put the chopped onion, garlic, ginger and around 60ml water into a food processor or blender and blitz to a purée, scraping down the sides every now and then.

Add the last tablespoon of oil to the hot pan. Scrape in the onion mixture and fry, stirring, until thickened and oil is seeping out of it. Add the ground spices except the garam masala, and fry for 30 seconds. Take off the heat and stir in the yoghurt, 1 tablespoon at a time.

Return to the heat, add the meat with its juices, stir, then pour in 400ml water and add salt. Simmer for 45–60 minutes until the lamb is very tender. Stir in the fried sliced onions and garam masala and simmer for another 2 minutes or so. Check the seasoning and serve.

thiou au poulet

Serves 6

12 boned chicken thighs

salt and freshly ground black pepper

1 heaped tablespoon coriander seeds

2 tablespoons sunflower or rapeseed oil

1 large onion, peeled and chopped

4 garlic cloves, peeled and chopped

4 chunky thyme sprigs

6 generous tablespoons tomato purée

300g new potatoes

2 sweet potatoes

4 medium carrots

1 white cabbage

A thiou is a big Senegalese stew, flavoured with crushed coriander and thyme. It's straightforward and tastes very good. Serve it over rice to soak up all the juice.

Season the chicken with salt and pepper and set aside. Coarsely crush the coriander seeds, using a pestle and mortar. Heat the oil in a large casserole and gently fry the onion and garlic until tender. Add the thyme and coriander and stir around, then add the chicken pieces and fry for a further 5 minutes or so, turning and stirring fairly constantly.

Now stir in the tomato purée and add enough water to cover the chicken by about 4cm. Season with salt and pepper and bring up to the boil. Reduce the heat and simmer gently for 30–40 minutes.

Meanwhile, peel and thickly slice the potatoes, sweet potatoes and carrots. Cut the cabbage into 8 wedges. Add these vegetables to the casserole, pressing them down under the cooking liquid. If absolutely necessary, add a little more hot water so that the vegetables are barely covered. Simmer for another 15–20 minutes until the potatoes are cooked through. Taste and adjust the seasoning and serve over rice.

The oldest cookbook in the world is a hefty tome. It was written an impressive 4,000 thousand years ago. There's one copy only, tightly etched onto three clay tablets, found in what was once Mesopotamia, now Iraq. The recipes are surprisingly complex, and are characterised by a considerable number of seasonings, from garlic and mint to fish sauce, and of course, spices, most notably cumin.

cumin

Here is one enticing example. Ingredients: lamb, fat, onions, vinegar, beer, rocket, coriander, samidu (possibly a type of flour), cumin, beetroot, garlic and leeks. Method: cook the whole lot in one large pot until soft and mushy. Mmm – must try it. I have paraphrased and abbreviated, but the gist of the recipe remains true.

Cumin, like coriander, is native to the Eastern Mediterranean, growing wild in an arc that sweeps around from Egypt to Turkey. Its name still anchors it firmly to that region, barely changed since it was inscribed in ancient Akkadian, the language of that first cookbook. They called it *kamunu*, we call it cumin.

It won't come as a shock then, to realise that it surfaces in the Bible, too. In Isaiah we are told that '…the fitches (a kind of legume) are not threshed with a threshing instrument, neither is a cart wheel turned about upon the cumin; but the fitches are beaten out with a staff, and cumin with a rod.' In other words, you don't use machinery to separate fitches, or cumin seed from the chaff. You have to take it gently, beating it with a stick, so that the grains are not damaged. The reason I mention this particular paragraph is that it illustrates a noticeable similarity to modern-day cumin processing.

The cumin plant is an unremarkable specimen. It looks a little like cow parsley – about the same height, with a white umbrella-spoke flower head that is sometimes too heavy for the stalk, bowing it down towards the ground. In ideal conditions, i.e. warm, not burning hot, it starts to flower around 8 weeks after planting, producing mature seeds 6–8 weeks later. These are ready to harvest when the leaves are on the verge of giving up altogether, ready to die off now their work is done.

The whole plant is pulled up manually, then left to semi-dry on the threshing floor. Then they beat the hell out of it, usually by hand with rods to dislodge all the seeds. All very Biblical… Even if it's happening in India or Iran, or Morocco or Guatemala or any one of the many countries where cumin is grown. Actually, there are now perfectly good cumin-threshing machines but they are too expensive for all but large-scale cultivators.

Ancient Greeks and Romans kept pots of ground cumin on their dining tables, just as we do salt and pepper, and just as Moroccans do to this day. But the Roman author Pliny the Elder (the one who died trying to save a friend from Pompeii as Vesuvius boiled over) knew of other, less obvious uses for it. It was helpful in calming flatulence, but more memorably cumin could give you an unhealthy pallor. Young students, who had been dilly-dallying instead of working, swallowed cumin before tutorials, so that their pale drawn skin suggested hours of dedicated studiousness. ➥

zhug

This searingly hot relish comes originally from the Yemen. It's the tomato ketchup of the country, always on the meal table, ready to spice up whatever else arrives. Now, I am told, it is all the rage in Israel too, served up with grilled meats or fish, or stirred into soups and stews to give them a big kick of energy.

Serves 8

4 green chillies, deseeded and roughly chopped

5 large garlic cloves, peeled and roughly chopped

2 teaspoons ground cumin

½ teaspoon salt

60g coriander leaves, roughly chopped

8 cardamom pods

3–4 tablespoons extra virgin olive oil

Put all the ingredients, except the cardamom and oil, into a food processor. Slit open each cardamom pod, extract the seeds and crush these, then add to the processor. Blitz until everything is very finely chopped and evenly combined. Scrape the mixture out into a bowl and beat in the olive oil.

NOTE The super-fast whirring of the processor's blades has a nasty tendency to bring out the bitterness in olive oil, so for a truer, more rounded flavour, I stir the oil in after processing.

muhummara

Serves 6

4 red peppers

2 red chillies

100g walnuts, toasted

40g white bread, ripped into small pieces

2 teaspoons ground cumin

2 garlic cloves, peeled and chopped

1 tablespoon pomegranate molasses

salt

150ml extra virgin olive oil

Muhummara is a kissing cousin to hummus, a beautiful-brick red pepper and walnut spread laced with cumin and pomegranate molasses. Serve it with carrots, radishes, celery and so on, with warm Arab bread, or in sandwiches.

Preheat the grill to high. Grill the peppers and chillies until blackened and blistered all over, then drop into a plastic bag, seal and leave until cool enough to handle. Pull out the stems, then peel away the skins from the peppers and chillies. Quarter and deseed both.

Put the chillies and peppers into a food processor, along with all the remaining ingredients except the oil. Pulse until everything is fairly finely chopped. Now set the motor running constantly on a low speed and slowly pour in the olive oil.

Taste and adjust the seasoning – it needs more salt than you'd imagine. Scrape into a bowl; it's now ready to eat.

Such is the attraction of the spice, with that wonderful, aromatic scent tempered with a hint of armpit and bitterness, that it has travelled outwards – east and west, north and south – to take up an essential position in the food of many nations. Mexicans love cumin, Brazilians love cumin, the Congolese love cumin, so do the Tanzanians and the Moroccans and Iranians and so on, right over to India, Pakistan, Bengal and even parts of China. And so do I.

Using cumin

Cumin is by nature a savoury spice, boasting a characterful flavour. It can stand boldly alone, or take its place amongst a bevy of spices without overwhelming, or disappearing into the crowd. When I think of cumin, my mind turns first to the dishes of North Africa and the Middle East where it is used vigorously. It is so good in tagines and other stews, with lamb or chicken or even fish, and is essential in marinades for food to be grilled. Good, too, sprinkled onto grilled foods perhaps with a scattering of sumac for sharpness.

It is even better with pulses and vegetables, simmered into tomatoey vegetable dishes, or dusted over a bowl of baba ganoush (aubergine purée) or hummus. Add it – either ground or toasted and crushed – to salads and side dishes for an instant Arabic lift.

India produces and consumes more cumin than any other country – worth bearing in mind when you make your own curries. If you use ready-ground cumin, make sure it is fresh and lively and err on the side of generosity, or better still dry-fry and grind it yourself, especially for garam masala (see page 217) so you get the full Indian impact in your final dish.

Use it too for some of the more incidental dishes. Jeera rice is simply rice cooked pilau style, with onions and cumin seeds in it. Or dry-fry cumin and coriander seeds (in a ratio of 1:2) then grind and use as a seasoning on salads, adding a little cayenne for heat if you wish and a spritz of lime. In India this spice duo is known as dhana jeera powder (see page 210) and is sold ready blended. Exactly the same combination works wonders in many soups, or on roast, grilled or fried fish. I've added the cumin-coriander blend to fishcakes (together with chopped leaf coriander) and vegetable purées too. All of them are hugely enhanced by it.

For epic scrambled eggs, fry an onion in butter. When soft, add chopped garlic and ginger, and 1–2 teaspoons cumin seeds. Once they pop, reduce the heat, add beaten eggs and scramble as usual, seasoning to taste. Serve topped with a little chopped tomato and coriander. Sunday brunch doesn't get much better than that…

dukkah

Serves 4–6

Serves 4–6

30g hazelnuts

4 tablespoons sesame seeds

2 tablespoons coriander seeds

1½ tablespoons cumin seeds

½ tablespoon black peppercorns

2 teaspoons ground cinnamon

½ teaspoon salt, or to taste

Dukkah is a sublime blend of spices and seeds and, in this instance, nuts, all toasted and roasted to bring out their hidden depths, then ground to a rough powder. To enjoy it at its finest, serve with a bowl of excellent extra virgin olive oil. Dip sticks of pepper or celery or carrot, or little tomatoes or radishes first into the oil, then the dukkah, so that it clings on all the way into the mouth. Dukkah will also enliven grilled or roast foods, or plainly cooked vegetables. The flavours are at their best on the day the dukkah is ground, but it can be kept for several weeks in an airtight jar.

Preheat the oven to 180°C/Gas mark 4. Scatter the hazelnuts on a baking tray and toast in the oven for about 5 minutes, then tip onto a board and chop roughly.

Heat a small, heavy frying pan over a medium heat, add the sesame seeds and shake the pan gently until the seeds turn a shade darker and give out a nutty smell. Tip them into a bowl. Repeat with the coriander and cumin seeds. When cool, place the roasted sesame, coriander and cumin seeds in a spice grinder or clean coffee grinder with the peppercorns and grind to a coarse dry powder. Transfer to a bowl and mix with the cinnamon and salt.

Crush the hazelnuts in the grinder — but don't whiz them for long, or you will end up with a hazelnut butter instead of very finely chopped nuts. Add to the rest of the ingredients and toss to mix.

xinjiang lamb kebabs

Serves 4

600g lamb leg steaks

2 tablespoons sunflower oil

2 tablespoons soy sauce

2 tablespoons cumin seeds

3 garlic cloves, peeled and crushed

1 tablespoon dried chilli flakes

2 teaspoons freshly ground black pepper

2 teaspoons ground ginger

Most of us wouldn't associate cumin with Chinese cooking, but in Xinjiang in the west of the country, it is incredibly popular. These cumin and chilli lamb kebabs are a favourite street food, hot and bold and hard to resist.

Slice the lamb into pieces about 5cm long, 3cm wide, and a mere 5mm thick. This doesn't have to be exact, but you get a rough idea. Put the lamb into a bowl and add the sunflower oil and soy sauce.

Dry-fry the cumin seeds in a small frying pan over a medium heat until they begin to release their aroma. Tip into a mortar, cool, then crush roughly with the pestle. Add to the lamb, along with all the remaining ingredients. Cover and leave to marinate for at least an hour, and up to 24 hours.

Thread the pieces of lamb onto skewers as if you were sewing — push the skewer in near one end, then take it under and back through the meat, then through the meat again towards the end. Thread 4 or 5 at most onto each skewer.

Preheat the grill to high, or heat up the barbecue thoroughly. Grill the skewers for around 6–8 minutes, turning once. Eat while hot.

There was a handsome blue and white Chinese ginger jar on the shelf in my mother's larder. My mother adored syrupy stem ginger. The jar came out on special occasions – birthdays, guests, Boxing day – to take its place on the lazy Susan in the centre of our dining table. Alongside would be a dish full of ice cream, bowls of nuts and raisins and other delights. A do-it-yourself sort of a pudding, starring the sweet stinging stem ginger soaked in syrup, that we hoiked out of the ginger jar.

ginger

Not only the jar, but probably also the ginger inside it came from China. A fitting state of affairs, for ginger is believed to have originated in southern China. Ginger has been prized and cultivated for so many centuries that it no longer bears the slightest resemblance to anything growing in the wild, so it's hard to be sure of its start. It holds high status, celebrated not only as a masterly culinary ingredient, but also as a genuinely effective medicine. Fresh ginger tea, for instance, is known to soothe nausea and many digestive orders.

Dismayingly, it was these very qualities that enmeshed ginger in a deeply distressing episode in the early years of the last century. On the morning of 30th February 1930, a distraught man stumbled into Dr. Ephraim Goldfain's office. Something was badly wrong with his legs. At each step his foot flopped down, slapping toe first on the floor as his leg descended. He was just the first. On that day alone, five flop-toed patients turned up at Reconstruction Hospital, Oklahoma.

Much the same scene was being played out in doctor's offices right across the States, but it was Dr. Goldfain who finally pinpointed the cause. All the victims were knocking back copious quantities of Jamaican Ginger Extract, or 'jakes' as it was commonly known.

The popularity of jakes was hardly new. This was the prohibition era when alcoholic drinks were banned by law. Jamaican Ginger extract was a counter-top medicine, sold to soothe nausea and diarrhoea. Jamaican ginger was already considered some of the best in the world, but what attracted most of its consumers was the 70–80% alcohol in the extract.

What happened next was not the fault of the ginger growers or extractors. New laws decreed that the solids content of all medicines must be doubled, in order to make the taste too vile to gulp. In Boston Harry Gross, a dubious entrepreneur, discovered that if he mixed jakes with TOCP, a cheap chemical used to make plastics pliable, the solids increased, but you couldn't taste or see the adulteration. Bingo! The money came rolling in.

What he hadn't foreseen was the catastrophic effect this would have on regular drinkers. Within a few months, jake leg was a well-known affliction amongst the poor. Official figures record over 50,000 cases of full or partial irreversible paralysis. Harry Gross and his partner received a two-year suspended jail sentence.

Jamaican ginger cultivation survived this whole sorry story. To this day Jamaican ginger is considered the finest, most delicate of all gingers (there are an absurd number of cultivars out there), but production levels are lower than they once were. These days India is the largest producer of ginger in the world, closely followed by China and Indonesia. Hawaii has cornered the American market to a large extent, with beautiful blue-ringed ginger, said to be of remarkable flavour and juiciness. So, should you slice into a handsome hand of ginger, do not be dismayed if you find a strange blue-green halo around the heart. Shout with joy and slice or chop away with renewed enthusiasm. This is a mark of sterling quality.

In many ways, ginger is an easy crop to grow, as long as you happen to live in a humid tropical climate. All you need is a bit of the rhizome – that's what most of us call ginger root, though it is actually a swollen food-bearing subterranean stem. Plant it and lo and behold 5–6 months later there are handsome leaves waving around above ground, and underground a big haul of ginger rhizomes linked together in a tight fat tangle.

The Japanese are inclined to prefer rather younger, extra tender ginger, to slice and preserve as an accompaniment to sushi and sashimi, while those who extract ginger oil generally like their rhizomes a little older, more fibrous and far more pungent – strong enough to knock your socks off. ➥

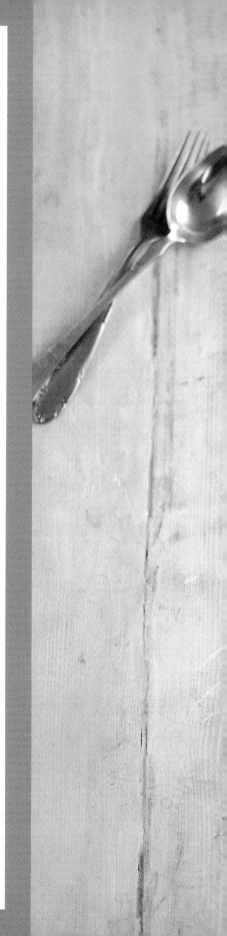

chinese cool ginger chicken

Serves 4–6

1 chicken, about 1.6kg

5cm piece fresh root ginger, peeled and
 roughly chopped

3 garlic cloves, peeled and sliced

7 spring onions, trimmed and roughly
 chopped

salt

100ml sunflower oil

1 tablespoon sesame oil

This is a pure, delicious way to cook and eat chicken when the weather is hot. You
must start with a good-quality free-range bird, but once that's sorted, the rest is plain
sailing. Not only will the meat be perfectly moist, you will also have a pot of gingery
chicken stock to use for a chicken noodle soup next day.

Settle the chicken, breast down, in a large deep saucepan and tuck a quarter of the ginger,
two-thirds of the garlic and a quarter of the spring onions around it. Add 1 teaspoon salt
and enough water to just cover the chicken. Bring slowly to the boil and simmer gently for
30 minutes. Now cover the pan, remove from the heat and leave the chicken to cool down
slowly in the cooking liquid.

Lift out the cooled chicken and cut into bite-sized pieces, discarding the skin and bones.

To make the dressing, put the remaining ginger, garlic and spring onions in a food
processor with ¼ teaspoon salt and process briefly until coarsely chopped. Transfer to
a bowl and stir in the sunflower oil and sesame oil. Spoon over the chicken and serve.

Ginger five ways

Fresh ginger Fresh ginger root is the new darling of cooks in the western world, as they delve deeper into Asian cooking. When buying it, pick out plump chunks with a taut, tan skin, no wrinkles and no discoloured soft patches, which suggest rot or mould. Look, too, at the cut ends. Slightly dry is fine and can be sliced off; verging on desiccated, on the other hand, suggests a dry interior and is best avoided.

The easiest and most effective way to peel fresh ginger is with a teaspoon. Try it and see. Just scrape the tip of the teaspoon along the ginger and the skin strips off, taking virtually none of the ginger with it.

Should you need to grate fresh ginger, it pays to pop the root in the freezer for a few hours first. As you grate, the frozen fibres in the ginger snap to give you a fine mound of ginger, instead of a tangled mass of fibres.

Dried ginger At specialist Asian food stores, particularly Chinese, you can buy whole chunks of dried root ginger. I've found these too hard to grind finely. Ginger is one of the rare spices that is better bought ready ground, at least for home use.

Ground or powdered ginger Poor old ground ginger has become something of a granny's spice, seen as old-fashioned beside fresh ginger root. A shame, as it is still just as good in baking as it ever was. Like all ground spices it loses aroma quite speedily, so buy little and often, discarding old tubs of discoloured, dulled ground ginger after 3–4 months.

Stem ginger in syrup and candied ginger You couldn't really call either of these a spice, but even so they are fine ingredients to keep in your store cupboard. Stem ginger is a startling and invigorating addition not only to sweet dishes, but also to many savoury ones.

Japanese pickled ginger Again, hardly a spice but yet another way to introduce the vigour of ginger to salads and fish dishes in particular. It is made with young tender root ginger, very thinly sliced then steeped in rice vinegar, sugar and salt. ➥

meen moolee

Serves 4

500g white fish fillets

salt

1 teaspoon ground turmeric

60g tamarind pulp

2 tablespoons sunflower oil

1 onion, peeled and thinly sliced

6 garlic cloves, peeled and thinly sliced

3cm piece fresh root ginger, peeled and
finely chopped

4 green chillies, halved lengthways and
deseeded

20 curry leaves (optional)

1 teaspoon ground cumin

1 teaspoon ground coriander

400g tin coconut milk

This Keralan fish curry with coconut and tamarind is pleasingly simple and quick
to prepare. It relies totally on the small gang of flavourings that go into it; fresh root
ginger is essential.

Tamarind is sold in two forms. In this recipe I've used the firm block form
that comes with seeds and fibres embedded in it. Asian food stores and some
supermarkets sell it like this. More common in larger supermarkets is ready-prepared
tamarind purée, an adequate substitute, but definitely second best.

Lay the fish fillets on a board. Mix ½ teaspoon salt with ½ teaspoon turmeric and rub over
the fish; set aside.

Put the tamarind into a bowl and pour over enough boiling water to cover. Leave to soften
for 10 minutes, then break it up and stir. Strain the tamarind through a sieve, pressing
through the soft pulp and leaving behind the fibres and seeds.

Heat the oil in a frying pan or wok over a medium heat and add the onion, garlic, ginger
and chillies. Fry gently until the onion is translucent, then add the curry leaves, if using, and
fry for another 2–3 minutes. Scoop out about 5 curry leaves and set aside to be used as
a garnish. Add the remaining turmeric along with the other ground spices and fry for a few
more minutes.

Pour in the coconut milk and tamarind purée and bring to the boil. Lower the heat and
simmer for 3–4 minutes, then add the fish. Simmer for a few minutes more until the fish
is cooked through.

Serve immediately, garnished with the reserved curry leaves.

Galangal Also known as Siamese ginger or blue ginger, galangal is closely related to ginger. It looks similar if a little smaller, but tastes very different. It's less pungent, more floral, but with a noticeably earthy, piny scent. It's frequently used in South-East Asian cooking. Confusingly, there are three different forms of galangal – greater, lesser and kaempfur – but in practice you usually just have to take what you can get. Most Asian supermarkets and the occasional deli or supermarket stock dried sliced or powdered galangal. If you are lucky you may come across grated galangal in oil, or better still fresh. Whatever form, it may be labelled *laos* or *kencur*.

Using ginger

Ginger goes with everything. However, don't imagine that you can swap one form with another willy-nilly. Dried powdered ginger tastes so very different to fresh ginger and is in no way inferior, even if it is less fashionable. It should be used where its particular virtues shine. So, there is no doubt that it belongs in the realms of cakes and biscuits, bringing a sensational warmth and tingle. Clever clogs sometimes replace it with fresh ginger, which is, by and large, a pointless exercise. Dried ginger is also very much at home in the tagines of Morocco, where it merges amiably with the mellow, rounded blends of spices. And as for drinks, what a huge haul there are when you chase ginger across the world: ginger beer and ginger ale, ginger wine, ginger-scented coffee, chai, and that's just the tip of the iceberg.

Fresh ginger, as you would expect, has a brighter, cleaner taste that instantly makes it a winner with fish, chicken, meat and vegetables. It lies at the heart of so many dishes – particularly Asian ones – that it is impossible to pick just one or two as examples. It takes pride of place in Chinese cooking, tossed into the wok right at the beginning of cooking with its constant companion garlic, but is just as essential to Japanese or South-East Asian cooks. In Africa, it is equally popular, in soups and stews and drinks galore.

In other words, if you enjoy cooking to any degree, make sure you always have a chunk of root ginger in your vegetable drawer, and a small jar of ground dried ginger in your spice cupboard.

sticky gingerbread

Makes 8–10 slices

280g plain flour

1 teaspoon bicarbonate of soda

1 tablespoon ground ginger

1 teaspoon ground cinnamon

¼ teaspoon salt

170g unsalted butter, softened

90g light muscovado sugar

220g golden syrup

1 egg

200ml milk

4 balls of preserved stem ginger, drained
and chopped

This is the gingerbread recipe I come back to time after time. It contains both ground and preserved stem ginger and is particularly moist, sticky and appealing. It's even better a day or two after it has been baked. If you're not eating it immediately, let it cool, then wrap in greaseproof paper, over-wrap with foil and store in an airtight tin.

Preheat the oven to 180°C/Gas mark 4. Line the base of a 20cm square cake tin with non-stick baking parchment and butter the sides. Mix the flour with the bicarbonate of soda, ground ginger, cinnamon and salt.

In a large bowl, cream the butter with the sugar until light and fluffy. Now beat in the golden syrup, then a heaped tablespoonful of the flour mixture followed by the egg. Beat in the remaining flour, followed by the milk to form a smooth batter. Stir in the stem ginger.

Scrape the mixture into the prepared tin and spread evenly. Bake for about 40–45 minutes until firm to the touch. Test by inserting a skewer deep into the centre; if it comes out clean then the gingerbread is done.

Let it cool in the tin for 15 minutes, then turn out onto a wire rack and leave to cool completely. Cut into slices or squares to serve.

Juniper is under threat. In Asia, the magnificent juniper forests of Baluchistan are in trouble. They are the largest on the planet, but grazing, disease and the need for firewood are gnawing away at them. Some of the trees are as much as two and a half millennia old – living fossils that want to carry on living. In California scrub fires sizzle and splutter their way through the junipers of the Mojave desert. And in the UK the juniper is having a tough time because of a lack of sex. How very British.

juniper

Now it's only right to point out that neither the *Juniperus macropoda* of Pakistan, nor the *Juniperus californica* of California produces the spice juniper. It's the third one, *Juniperus communi*s that is the culinary treasure. It grows right across Europe, America and Asia, in the cooler, more temperate parts. The sex issue is a tricky one. Juniper trees are dioecious, in other words both male and female plants are needed in order to produce viable seeds. So far so good. Unfortunately a large proportion of the female plants are well past their prime – they can live to some 200–300 years old – and their reproductive powers are on the wane. Fewer mature seeds results in fewer small plants, which means that ravenous bunnies and bambies are munching a greater proportion of the next generation of juniper bushes.

All is not lost, however. All around the world, conservation bodies are running projects to protect and replant junipers. I'm relieved. I'm prepared to give up my once-in-a-blue-moon juniper picking foray, but I wouldn't want to do without juniper berries altogether. Juniper is a rare cool weather spice, one that feels right at home in more northerly climes. It is a surprisingly oily spice, too. Crush a berry between your fingers and you'll see what I mean. Then take a good long smell. It's fruity, almost appley, laced with a resinous turpentine aroma, instantly recognisable as the keynote in gin. There's no other spice quite like it.

The berries themselves are not berries at all; they are, in fact, cones. Juniper is a conifer so there is a logic to this, but even so, the small blue-black fruit looks as unlike a pine cone as a fruit can look. It has a grand total of three scales that fuse together as the fruit matures. This happens at a phenomenally slow rate – it takes 2 years for a cone to mature fully.

The bulk of the juniper berries sold either to cooks, or more likely to distillers and brewers, are picked from the wild in Eastern Europe, particularly Macedonia. The traditional method is to spread sheets underneath the needled branches, then beat them with a rod to dislodge ripe fruit. Most of the harvest is heading for the drink. There's gin for the British, Borovicka for the Slovaks, Sahti for the Finns, Genever for the Dutch and plenty more where they come from.

From the juniper forests of Central Europe, the Brothers Grimm plucked one of their most gruesome stories, The Juniper Tree. A mother dies and is buried under the juniper trees near her house. Naturally, her grieving husband swiftly remarries so that his small son will be cared for. Naturally, the new wife is wicked. Eventually she decapitates the little boy, and turns his blood into black puddings, which they eat for their supper. You'll be glad to hear that ultimately she gets her come-uppance, smashed to a pulp by a millstone falling from the sky, and the boy comes back to life. And they all live happily ever after. Hurrah!

Notes on juniper

✿ Juniper berries are always sold whole, as far as I am aware. I suspect they are too oily and soft for commercial milling, but these are positive attributes in the domestic kitchen. It is easy to crush a juniper berry between finger and thumb, so if you are only using a small number of them that's as good a way as any.

✿ For a finer juniper mash, use a pestle and mortar, with coarse salt if you want to tear them to small specks. What you won't end up with is a fine powder. ❧

marinated mackerel salad

*Serves 8 as a first course,
  or 4 as a main course*

4 smoked mackerel fillets

juice of 1 lemon

2 teaspoons caster sugar

10 juniper berries, roughly crushed

2 wholemeal pitta breads

120g rocket leaves

200g cherry tomatoes, halved

2 tablespoons extra virgin olive oil

This is an old favourite of mine that I throw together frequently. The sweet-sharp juniper marinade gives the smoked mackerel a real lift.

Flake the mackerel fillets, discarding the skin and any stray bones you come across. Toss with the lemon juice, sugar and juniper berries and set aside for at least 1 hour.

Split the pitta breads in half and grill until crisp. Break into pieces.

Shortly before serving toss the rocket with the cherry tomatoes, mackerel and any juices, pitta bread pieces and olive oil. Divide between serving plates.

pheasant terrine

Serves 6–8

1 plump pheasant, including livers
   if available

2 tablespoons brandy

300g belly of pork, minced

180g veal, minced

10 juniper berries, crushed

finely grated zest of 1 lemon

2 shallots, peeled and very finely chopped

2 garlic cloves, peeled and very finely
   chopped

2 teaspoons thyme leaves

2 tablespoons chopped parsley

1 egg

6 tablespoons dry white wine

salt and freshly ground black pepper

about 220g sheet pork back fat, 3mm
   thick, or thinly sliced streaky bacon

6 or 7 bay leaves

A polite waft of juniper permeates this game pâté, making it a total treat for autumn or winter. Creating terrines and pâtés is much simpler than most people think. Buy the meats from a good butcher, so that they can mince them for you. If they are game dealers as well, they will skin the pheasant and remove the breasts too.

Skin the pheasant, then remove the breasts and cut these into slices, about 1cm thick. Place the slices in a bowl, add the brandy and leave to marinate for 2 hours.

Strip as much of the remaining flesh as you can from the pheasant carcass, discarding tough tendons and sinews. Chop the meat finely, and chop the livers finely too, if you have them. Now mix with the remaining ingredients, except the sheet of pork back fat and bay leaves, seasoning the mixture with salt and pepper. When the breast pieces have stoked up their allotted time in the brandy, drain off the juices and mix them in too.

Fry a small knob of the mixture in a small pan and then taste to check the seasoning. Adjust accordingly.

Preheat the oven to 170°C/Gas mark 3, and put the kettle on to boil. Line a 1 litre terrine with the pork back fat. Cut a few strips from the rest to decorate the top.

Spread one-third of the minced meat mixture over the base of the lined terrine, then arrange half of the marinated pheasant breast slices over that. Repeat these layers, then dollop on the rest of the pâté mixture. Smooth firmly, mounding it up gently. Arrange the strips of pork fat and bay leaves prettily on top.

Cover the dish with a rectangle of greased foil. Stand in a roasting tin, and pour enough very hot water around the dish to come about 2.5cm up the sides. Cook in the oven for 1½–2 hours until the pâté is just firm to the touch and shrinking well away from the sides of the dish, removing the foil for the last 20 minutes so that the top can brown a little.

Lift the terrine out of the roasting tin, cover with a new sheet of foil and weight down with a couple of tins. Once the terrine is cool, transfer to the fridge until needed.

Serve thickly sliced, with cornichons, pickled walnuts and/or a good vibrant fruit chutney, and great bread.

Using juniper

I think juniper, I think game, I think highlands of Scotland, I think Monarch of the Glen. There is something utterly right about the pairing of piney, powerful juniper with venison, and with a good dose of red wine or port for the marinade or gravy. The trouble with such an obvious and powerful combination is that it can overshadow the wider possibilities.

Juniper is a sensational flavouring for wild boar or a slow-roast plump shoulder of free-range pork, too. Occasionally I like to take it to extremes, cooking the joint – smeared generously with crushed juniper berries and barded with slivers of garlic and chilli – for a full 24 hours at a low temperature. (Start at 220°C/Gas mark 7 for 30 minutes to crisp the skin, then reduce the setting to 110°C/Gas mark ½ for the next 23½ hours, basting occasionally; rest for half an hour before serving.)

However, juniper is not only a meat enhancer. Oh no. Juniper is a far more versatile spice than we give it credit for, and although it is relatively strong in flavour, it can be used more generously than you might imagine.

Quite besides being an essential element in gin, juniper has a great affinity with pâtés and sausages of all kinds, the piney flavour cutting through fattiness and supporting the rich meaty flavours. In Germany it is an important ingredient in sauerkraut, bringing a lingering smokiness to preserved cabbage.

Juniper is terrifically good with oily fish, softening the richness of mackerel or salmon. Use it in a marinade for either fish, crushing it with sea salt, then stirring in lemon juice, pepper and lemon zest. Or make a small stuffing of breadcrumbs, juniper, lime or lemon, butter, salt and pepper, to fill the cavity of whole fish. Even more straightforward, merely fill the central cavity with bruised juniper berries, or lay the fish on a bed of juniper branches, slipping another twig inside, then bake in a hot oven until cooked through. If you ever make your own gravid lax – easy and so effective – add crushed juniper berries and a slug of gin to the curing mix to impart an aromatic Scandinavian flavour.

For a more unexpected but welcome combination, turn to chocolate. Add a few crushed juniper berries to brownies, or chocolate fondant puddings for a more grown-up, elusive aroma.

petits pots au chocolat

Serves 4

300ml single cream

9 juniper berries, crushed

3 egg yolks

30g caster sugar

100g dark chocolate, or high-quality milk
    chocolate, roughly chopped

To serve (optional):

a little whipped cream

Actually creamy chocolate cups scented with juniper... and what a joy they are. The fruity, resinous tang of juniper works a little magic on chocolate puds, and this one is no exception. Chocolate purists will make them with deeply dark chocolate (some 70% cocoa solids) but I prefer the taste a little gentler and softer, and make them with a good-quality milk chocolate (37–40% cocoa solids). No one has complained yet.

Preheat the oven to 140°C/Gas mark 1. In a heavy-based pan, slowly bring the cream and juniper almost to a simmer, then turn the heat right down, half-cover the pan and leave to infuse for 10 minutes. If you can't lower the heat enough to stop the cream simmering, then turn off the heat and cover. Meanwhile, in a bowl, beat together the egg yolks and sugar.

Take the cream pan off the heat and stir in the chocolate. Keep stirring until it has fully melted. Pour the hot chocolate cream onto the egg yolk mixture, whisking constantly.

Strain the mixture into a jug, and pour into 4 small ramekins or espresso cups. Stand them in a roasting tin and pour enough boiling water around them to come 1cm up their sides.

Slide into the oven and cook for 45 minutes until just set, but still slightly soft in the centre. Lift out of the roasting tin and leave to cool, then chill until needed.

Bring the petits pots back to room temperature before serving. Top each one with a small swirl of whipped cream if you wish.

As saffron is the most expensive spice in the world – at times it's been worth more than its weight in gold – you might have thought farmers would be queuing to get their hands on saffron corms. You'd be wrong. Over recent decades there has been a drastic decline in saffron growing across the world. In Spain, once the king of saffron, production has plummeted from 6,000 hectares in the 1970s to 100 hectares today, a mere pimple on the great plains of Castilla-La Mancha.

saffron

It's a different story in France, and even more different in Afghanistan, where there's something of a resurgence in saffron cultivation. A couple of years ago, I came across a brave, some might even say foolish, couple at a food festival in rural France. Their stall announced loudly that they were growing saffron just a few miles away. Early years, and the yield was still small and experimental, not enough to market as a pure spice yet. Instead they were making their own exceptional jams and jellies, all flavoured with their own, hand-picked red gold. Wonderful stuff.

They are not alone. There are dozens of small saffron growers in France, perhaps most notably around Boynes, which was once considered the absolute centre of the world saffron trade. Every autumn morning the saffron fields, radiating out around the town into the countryside, awoke purple with crocus flowers. At first light, women were out with their baskets, plucking the blooms singly before insects could nibble their way in, before the warmth of sunlight seduced the petals to open wide. It was painstaking, back-wrenching, relentless work. By midday they would be sitting down together, around a table piled high with purple, nipping out the rust-red stigmas of each flower, one by one. Repetitive, tedious, fiddly work that had to be completed before anyone could go to bed.

In the 1880s, the Boyne saffron fields were decimated – first by two appallingly severe winters, then by increasing labour costs and the gradual migration of the young to easier jobs in the towns. The last of the old *safraniers* closed business in 1930. But now there's a proud new saffron museum, and the young are returning to the old saffron trade.

Saffron corms (resembling bulbs, but technically swollen basal stems) like moderation: moderately good soil, moderate rainfall, moderate temperatures. For most of the year the fields look dull and lifeless. Then as autumn sets in, the air begins to cool and the snoozing corms wake, poking up skewer-thin leaves. In October, the first of the purple flowers appear. At the heart of each flower are the yellow stamen, the male pollen bearing parts, and the red gold itself, the three stigma, joined at their base to the style, which connects them directly to the flower's ovary.

Though Afghanistan is about as different as you can get from rural France or Spain, saffron growing is one of the new weapons employed in transforming the economy. Saffron appreciates a similar climate to the opium poppy and is one of the few crops that can compete in terms of profit. The quality is high, but so are the stakes. The Taliban have destroyed saffron fields in a bid to reinstate the opium poppies that they can profit from. It's a no-win situation for the farmers: grow saffron and it is destroyed by one side, grow opium and it's destroyed by the other.

The biggest saffron producer in the world by far is Iran, which now grows over 90% of the world's supply. It exports a mere 100 tonnes a year, give or take, not really a great deal, until you consider that it takes an area the size of a football field to produce half a kilo of saffron.

You could quite easily grow your own saffron, and no, you don't need a football field to do it. Most of us use tiny amounts of saffron every year, so a generous handful or two of saffron crocus bulbs, planted at the end of the garden, would be quite adequate. All you need do is pluck the flowers as soon as they emerge in the autumn, carefully remove the stigma, and let them dry on muslin for a day or two. It's a wonder that more of us don't do it. ➥

mouclade

Serves 4

large pinch of saffron threads

1 tablespoon hot water

2kg fresh mussels

60g butter, softened

1 tablespoon plain flour

1 large onion, peeled and chopped

150ml dry white wine

1 teaspoon medium curry powder

250g crème fraîche

salt and freshly ground black pepper

chopped parsley, to serve

This lovely mussel dish, enriched with crème fraîche and gilded with saffron and a touch of curry, is from the west coast of France. Curry sounds oddly ungallic, but it arrived in Atlantic ports on trading ships returning from the east, and was swiftly appropriated as a seasoning. You can clean the mussels and make the beurre manié in advance, but don't cook the mussels or finish the sauce until you're ready to serve.

Soak the saffron in the hot water for at least 30 minutes. Meanwhile, clean the mussels under cold running water, tugging away the beards. Discard any mussels with cracked shells, and any that are open and fail to shut when rapped on the edge of the sink. Once cleaned, rinse again in a sink full of clean water to get rid of as much grit as possible.

Mash half the butter with the flour to form a beurre manié. Heat the remaining butter in a frying pan and fry the onion gently until tender.

Meanwhile, bring the wine to the boil in a large saucepan. Tip in the mussels, clamp the lid on tight and steam over a high heat, shaking the pan frequently, until virtually all the mussels have opened — this should take at most 5 minutes, probably less. Discard any that stay closed. Tip the mussels and juice into a sieve set over a bowl. Once drained, transfer the mussels to a warm serving bowl, cover and keep warm while you finish the sauce.

When the onion is tender, stir in the curry powder and cook for another minute. Carefully pour in the liquid from the mussels, leaving any grit in the bowl. Add the saffron water and stir in the crème fraîche and some salt and pepper. Bring to the boil, stirring. Lower the heat and stir in small knobs of beurre manié until the mixture is nicely thickened (you may not need it all). Let the sauce cook quietly for another minute or so.

Tip the sauce over the warm mussels, sprinkle with parsley and serve at once.

moroccan tagine of chicken with preserved lemons

Serves 4

1 free-range chicken, about 1.6kg

1 teaspoon ground turmeric

1 teaspoon ground ginger

1 teaspoon ground cumin

4 garlic cloves, peeled and crushed

salt and freshly ground black pepper

1 onion, peeled and grated

2 chicken livers (optional)

1 tablespoon extra virgin olive oil

300ml water, plus 1 tablespoon

large pinch of saffron threads

1 preserved lemon

110g Moroccan pink green olives,
  or other plump green olives

This is possibly my favourite Moroccan tagine of all. It brings together three top ranking ingredients – salty olives, aromatic preserved lemon and golden saffron. Dynamite!

Traditionally, tagines are served on their own, with good bread to mop up the juices, but I love a tagine with couscous, too, even if it is most inauthentic. The preserved lemons, however, cannot be replaced with anything else. Luckily, most good delis and some larger supermarkets stock preserved lemons these days.

Trim the flaps of excess fat from the chicken at the opening to the body cavity, and remove any other lumps of fat you can locate. Truss the bird firmly, by tucking the ends of the legs into the opening, and tying them in place with string. Rub the turmeric, ginger and cumin over the chicken, and then smear over half the garlic. Season lightly with salt and pepper. Cover and leave to marinate in the fridge for up to 12 hours.

Put the onion, remaining garlic, the chicken livers (if using), olive oil and 300ml water into a flameproof casserole or tagine large enough to take the chicken. Stir and bring up to the boil. Now add the chicken, and reduce the heat so that the liquid is barely simmering. Cover the pan, leaving just a small gap for steam to escape, and cook for 1¾–2 hours, turning the chicken frequently so that the flesh is partially steamed and partially simmered to a melting tenderness.

Meanwhile, soak the saffron in 1 tablespoon hot water. Scrape the pulp out of the lemon and discard. Cut the peel into strips, rinse thoroughly, drain and reserve. Bring a pan of water to the boil. Rinse the olives, add to the boiling water and blanch for 1 minute to remove excess salt, then drain.

When it is done, take the chicken out of the casserole and keep warm. Find the livers, if using, quarter and reserve these too. Stir the saffron liquid, strips of preserved lemon and the olives into the remaining sauce in the pan, then simmer for 2–3 minutes. Taste and adjust the seasoning.

Serve the chicken with the sauce spooned over and around it, scattering the bits of liver in amongst the olives and lemon.

Notes on saffron

✪ A word of warning: do not be seduced by a holiday souvenir of cheap saffron. There is no such thing. Saffron is always expensive. Not only because of vast labour costs, but also because it is a crop that can be wiped out in a shake by bad weather.

✪ If you are wise, you will always buy saffron threads. The very best 'coupe' or 'sargol' grade (depending on origin) is a beautiful dark red tangle of threads. Second best saffron is streaked with a little yellow – the top part of the style that holds the three stigma together. It is light on flavour, so dampens the impact of the spice. One more step down is saffron streaked with yellow and white – the lower section of the style. This further diminishes the strength of the saffron.

✪ Powdered saffron is easily adulterated. Even with a reputable dealer or brand, the essential oils will evaporate swiftly once the threads are powdered, so unless you are using it all at once, it is not worth your money. Unscrupulous dealers will have no qualms about cutting powdered saffron with safflower or marigold petals, at best.

✪ In recipes saffron threads are usually measured in pinches, which is incredibly vague. I have seen recipes that instruct you to count out the threads, but personally I have better things to do with my time. The advantage of the 'pinch' is that you can personalise it. If you adore saffron then your pinch will be generous, if you are more cautious, then go for a restrained pinch. Either way, that pinch is generally speaking, enough for a dish for 6–8 people.

✪ There are several ways to prepare saffron for cooking. The most common is infusion. Put whole threads in a small ramekin or bowl and pour over a tablespoon or two of warm water, or milk, or other liquid. Leave it to steep for at least 30 minutes before using. If you are good at thinking ahead, you will get even better results if you soak your saffron overnight, or for 24 hours.

✪ Alternatively, grind your saffron to a powder – dry-fry it for a few brief seconds to crisp it up, then grind to a powder with a pestle and mortar and and add it straight to dishes as it is (a good option when there is little liquid in the recipe), or infuse in warm water or wine to give an even wash of gold.

✪ Saffron is usually added towards the end of cooking, to conserve all of its aroma. ❧

cornish saffron buns

Makes 12

2 large pinches of saffron threads

60ml hot water

500g strong white bread flour

½ teaspoon salt

200g unsalted or slightly salted butter,
    diced

80g caster sugar

7g sachet easy-blend dried yeast

220g mixed raisins, currants and sultanas

45g mixed candied orange and lemon
    peel, chopped

about 170ml milk

To finish:

a little extra milk

demerara sugar

Saffron buns are a European speciality, embraced with enthusiasm in Scandinavia and in Cornwall. Legend has it that the Phoenicians brought saffron to the Cornish, way before the Romans, but it seems more likely that they took up saffron cultivation in the 11th century when battle-worn crusaders came home with all manner of trophies, amongst them saffron corms. In Essex, another county where saffron growing was important, they retain the name in Saffron Walden, while in Cornwall they keep the habit of making and eating saffron buns.

The butter-enriched dough needs plenty of time and warmth to rise (if too cold, the butter congeals, holding the dough solid and barely capable of movement). If the weather is on the chilly side, put the dough in the airing cupboard to rise.

Dry-fry the saffron threads in a heavy-based frying pan over a moderate heat for a few seconds to toast them. Tip into a bowl and leave to cool slightly, then crumble the threads roughly. Add the hot water and leave to steep for at least an hour, or better still, overnight.

Mix the flour with the salt in a large bowl. Rub in the butter, using your fingertips, then add the sugar, yeast, dried fruit and candied peel. Pour in the infused saffron liquid and enough milk to form a soft, but not sticky dough. Knead the dough in the bowl for a good 10 minutes until smooth and elastic. Cover with a damp tea towel, then leave to rise in a warm place until doubled in bulk. As the dough is so rich, this will take much longer than you might expect even in a warm spot – say 3–4 hours.

Punch the dough down, knead again briefly and then divide into 12 pieces. Flour your hands lightly and roll each one into a ball. Place on greased baking trays, leaving plenty of room for each one to expand. Cover again with a damp tea towel and leave to rise once more in a warm place, until doubled in bulk. This time allow around 2 hours.

If, however, you want to cook the buns first thing in the morning, time proceedings so that you can leave them to rise overnight, in a comparatively cool place. If they still seem a bit small in the morning, quickly sit the tray of buns on top of a warmed hot water bottle to give them a bit of encouragement.

Preheat the oven to 180°C/Gas mark 4. Bake the buns for 20–25 minutes, until golden brown. As you take them from the oven, quickly brush the tops with milk, sprinkle with demarera sugar and return to the oven for a final 3–4 minutes. Cool on a wire rack.

Using saffron

Saffron goes with seafood, meat, poultry, creamy sauces and puddings, rice, sweet buns and breads. Recipes for saffron with cheese, pulses, vegetables and fruit exist, but they are comparatively thin on the ground. This does not necessarily mean they're to be avoided. In the past, saffron was the preserve of the rich, and even then it was used to impress and show off. And this meant using it to gild and scent the more expensive flashy foods. The cheap stuff – vegetables, lentils, blackberries and apples – were not smart enough, therefore no saffron.

In other words this is a spice you can be adventurous with, assuming that you like its strange, aromatic, almost metallic taste. I love discovering saffron in a Mediterranean-style dish of chickpeas and vegetables, or in a plate of Asian saffron and chilli potatoes. Saffron mashed potatoes (steep the saffron in the milk) look sunny and appealing, and even more golden if you mix in fresh, lightly cooked sweetcorn. Another way to introduce saffron to vegetables is to grind the saffron to a powder then dissolve it in melted butter to spoon over the cooked drained vegetables. Or make your own infused saffron oil to use in salad dressings with white wine vinegar, a pinch or two of sugar, salt and pepper.

Wherever saffron grows, so too do saffron recipes. From Spain comes the famous paella, too often coloured with food dye these days, while Marseilles bouillabaisse is always seasoned with saffron. It's fish and saffron again in Italy, but across the Med saffron is an ingredient in a handful of tagines, with rice, and in many of the luscious perfumed rice and milk puddings.

Sweeping up towards India, the same themes resurface again and again, the saffron shining in dishes that once graced royal tables – dishes in the style of the Mogul court (see page 169) or Shrikand (see page 171). Since both of these demand a certain amount of waiting around, you might prefer to throw together this very quick, very simple pudding instead: infuse saffron threads in a little warm cream for an hour or two, then beat into fresh ricotta together with some caster sugar, orange zest and raisins. Divide between small bowls and serve. Very good.

saffron lime macaroons

Makes 14

2 large pinches of saffron threads

180g icing sugar

120g ground almonds

3 large egg whites

80g caster sugar

Lime icing:

juice of ½ lime

2–3 drops of green food colouring
(optional)

80–100g icing sugar, sifted

So fashionable and so very good, French-style macaroons are easy to make. Saffron gives these a subtle, sophisticated aspect, while the lime in the icing cuts through the sweetness. They make a great present, if you can bear to give them away.

Line two baking trays with baking parchment. Using a small glass or a biscuit cutter, 4cm in diameter, as a guide, draw 14 circles on each sheet of parchment. Turn the paper over.

Dry-fry the saffron for a few seconds only, then crush to a powder; set aside. Blitz the icing sugar and ground almonds in a food processor to an even finer powder, then sift.

In a large bowl, whisk the egg whites with the powdered saffron to stiff peaks. Sprinkle over half the caster sugar and whisk until glossy. Add the remaining caster sugar and whisk for a few more minutes until you have a wonderfully thick, shiny golden meringue mixture. Now fold in the icing sugar/almond powder, using a large metal spoon, to make a thick batter.

Put the mixture into a piping bag fitted with a 1cm nozzle. Holding the nozzle upright, pipe directly down onto the centre of each circle, so that it spreads neatly out to the edges. Now leave them on the work surface for half an hour; a light skin will form on the surface.

Preheat the oven to 150°C/Gas mark 2. Bake the macaroons for 15–20 minutes until just firm. Try peeling one off the paper. If it sticks badly, bake them for a further 3–4 minutes or so. Once cooked, leave on the baking trays for a minute, then transfer to wire racks to cool.

To make the icing, mix the lime juice with the colouring, if using, and beat in enough icing sugar to make a thick, smooth icing. Sandwich the macaroons together with the icing and serve. Those that aren't for eating straight away can be stored in an airtight box in the fridge.

caraway

fennel

star anise

anise spices

Caraway has been hanging around for aeons. It is indigenous to an area that stretches from northern Africa right across to western Asia and has long been recognised as a useful spice and medicine. Stone Age man was already on the case; the Swiss paleobotanist Oswald Heer discovered remains of caraway seeds amongst the household goods preserved in the stone age lake dwellings at Robenhausen, near Zurich. They were found alongside remains of corn, barley and crab apples.

caraway

A couple of millennia later, the Egyptian Ebers Papyrus, an earnest medical treatise listing endless ways to alleviate greater and lesser suffering, commends caraway. It was inscribed in 1536 BC, and by then physicians had realised that caraway was pretty efficacious at dispelling trapped wind. Knock up a little caraway infusion and that 'bloated feeling' as it is so decorously described in modern TV ads could be soothed away, whilst simultaneously sweetening your breath. A double deal of pharaonic proportion.

The wind issue has remained on the agenda ever since. Turn to any of the subsequent herbals, from Pliny's *Naturalis Historiae* through the 16th century *Banckes' Herbal* to Mrs. M. Grieve's *A Modern Herbal* and the subject reappears as regular as clockwork. Even royalty suffers from time to time, though courtiers are surely prohibited from commenting. Woe betide anyone who dares to crack joke at the regal behind's expense. This may have given Anne Boleyn an early advantage with her King Henry. Legend has it that she drew his attention by offering him caraway comfits to ease his stomach. Irritable bowel syndrome? Over-eating? Who knows, but it seemed do the trick.

Culpeper also mentions them: 'Caraway Comfects, once only dipped in Sugar, and half a spoonful of them eaten in the morning fasting, and as many after each meal is a most admirable Remedy for such as are troubled with Wind.'

Caraway comfits, in other words sugar-coated caraway seeds, are still available today if you search around. My mum kept round yellow comfits in the larder, using them to decorate, amongst other things, the Christmas lemon soufflé that always appeared as an alternative to the flaming pudding. Not enough of them, unfortunately, to combat the effects of seasonal overindulgence.

We may have lost the habit of chewing on caraway comfits in the West, but in India and Indian restaurants abroad you will often find sugar-jacketed caraway, aniseed or fennel seeds in the saucer of spices proffered at the end of a meal.

There are two forms of caraway plant. One is an annual and requires a relatively long growing season, while the second, a biennial, is better adapted to a cooler climate. It employs the first year of its life in gaining strength and height (up to 70cm), then gets going on flowers and seeds in year two. The seeds are dark brown, curved and small, about half the size of a fennel seed. Like fennel seeds, caraway belongs to the Umbelliferae family and is similarly laced with liquorice, but don't let that put you off if you loathe liquorice, as I do – the flavour is low-key. The carrot is also a family member, and the two plants look similar, with their feathery leaves and umbels of small white flowers. Caraway even has an edible carrot-like tap root, which I am told is good to eat.

Cooking with caraway

The taste of caraway is surprisingly adaptable. Germany's cooks use it with all sorts of things. It goes into sauerkraut, that wonderful sour pickled cabbage, but it is also sprinkled on pork roasts, or added to a potato salad, or used with beetroot. The latter is a particularly inspired combination, especially if a little soured cream or mayonnaise is included. I like to serve very lightly blanched cabbage tossed with caraway seeds and a little melted butter, or stir the seeds into a homemade coleslaw. German and Scandinavian rye bread often contains the spice too.

Caraway works well with fish, and has a special affinity with cheeses, either to season creamy cheese (see right), or added to the curds at the dairy to flavour matured cheeses like Gouda or Hvarti.

North Africa brings more exotic recipes to the fore, particularly in the cuisine of Tunisia, where it is an essential element in tabil – a coriander, caraway and garlic spice blend. In the UK it stars in the wonderful, old-fashioned seed cake (page 126), as well as other baked goods. Try sprinkling caraway seeds amongst the filling for an apple pie, or with other lightly cooked fruit.

caraway & black pepper goat's cheese

Serves 6–8

400g soft goat's cheese

1 tablespoon cream or milk

½ red onion, peeled and very finely
  chopped

1 teaspoon caraway seeds, toasted and
  coarsely crushed

¼ teaspoon crushed black pepper

1 tablespoon chopped parsley

salt

The lick of caraway is a lovely addition to soft goat's cheese. Serve piled into a bowl, with crudités and/or warm pitta bread or pumpernickel, for an appetising first course. Or for a simple canapé, pile into the curves of short lengths of celery, or the curvier end of chicory leaves.

Just mix everything together in a bowl, seasoning with a pinch of salt, then taste and adjust the seasonings. Serve as a dip, or in celery sticks or chicory leaves, or spread on pumpernickel.

salade mechouia

Serves 3–4

500g ripe tomatoes

2 red peppers

1 green pepper

2 red Fresno or jalapeño chillies

2 garlic cloves, peeled and crushed

1 teaspoon caraway seeds, toasted and roughly crushed

juice of ½ large lemon

2 tablespoons extra virgin olive oil

pinch of sugar (optional)

1 tablespoon chopped parsley

salt and freshly ground black pepper

To serve:

12 black olives

2 eggs, hard-boiled, shelled and quartered (optional)

200g tin tuna in oil, drained and flaked (optional)

Arab breads, warmed

Tunisian cooks use a surprising amount of caraway and there is nowhere it works better than in this gorgeous salad of grilled tomatoes and peppers. It's not a salad as we know it, but a finely chopped and mulched amalgam of smoky summer vegetables, bordering on a purée, but retaining lots of texture.

You can serve it in all sorts of ways: as a side dish (leave out the egg and tuna), with fish or chicken, as a starter (with or without the egg and tuna), or turn it into a proper main course with all the garnishes, plus lots of warm bread, a green salad and a potato or rice salad as well.

Preheat the grill to high, or better still heat up the barbecue until white hot. Grill or barbecue the whole tomatoes, peppers and chillies until their skins are blackened and blistered all over. Carefully transfer the tomatoes to a bowl. Put the peppers and chillies into a plastic bag, seal and leave until cool enough to handle.

Peel the tomatoes, cut in half and scrape out the seeds. Pull the skins off the peppers and chillies and discard their stalks and seeds, saving as much of the juice as you can. Now pile the tomatoes, peppers and chillies on a board, get your largest knife and chop the whole lot together until you have a coarsely chopped mush.

Scrape the mixture into a bowl, adding the juices. Stir in the garlic, caraway, lemon juice, olive oil, sugar if using, chopped parsley, and some salt and pepper. Taste and adjust the seasonings.

Spoon the salad into a shallow serving plate and scatter over the olives. Garnish with hard-boiled egg quarters and tuna flakes if using. Eat the salad at room temperature with warm Arab bread to scoop it up.

old-fashioned seed cake

Serves 6–8

2 large eggs

unsalted butter

caster sugar

ground almonds

self-raising flour

1 teaspoon baking powder

2 heaped teaspoons caraway seeds

pinch of salt

1–2 tablespoons milk (if needed)

You don't see seed cake around much these days and that's a downright shame. It is the perfect everyday teatime cake. There's nothing grand or fancy about it – just an honest, homely, buttery taste that is accentuated by the dark flecks of caraway.

My version is based on a quatre-quarts cake. In other words you begin by weighing your eggs, which gives you the quantity of flour, butter and sugar you'll need.

Preheat the oven to 180°C/Gas mark 4. Line a 22x10cm loaf tin with baking parchment, or grease and flour it. Weigh the eggs and make a note of their weight. Weigh out the same quantity of butter and of sugar. Now for a bit of maths: divide the weight of the eggs by three. Weigh out this amount of ground almonds, then weigh out twice that amount of self-raising flour.

Melt the butter and cool until tepid. Mix the flour, ground almonds, baking powder, sugar, caraway seeds and salt together in a large bowl and make a well in the centre. Break in the eggs and then pour in the butter. Mix to a smooth batter with a dropping consistency, adding a little milk if needed.

Scrape the mixture into the prepared tin, smooth down lightly, then bake for 50–60 minutes until firm to the touch. To test to see if the cake is done, plunge a skewer into the centre; if it comes out clean, then the cake is ready. If not, return to the oven for another 5–10 minutes.

Leave the cake in the tin for 10 minutes, then turn out and cool on a wire rack. Serve warm or cool, on its own or spread with a little butter.

'...He flung down his shield
Ran like fire once more: and the space 'twixt the fennel-field
And Athens was stubble again, a field which a fire runs through,
Till in he broke: "Rejoice, we conquer!"'

fennel

That's Robert Browning's spin on the last heroic run of Pheippides, Greek herald, soldier and phenomenal speedmeister. The Greek army, headed up by Miltiades, was based 42km from Athens, and they knew that the massive Persian army was hell bent on destroying them. Pheippides ran and ran all the way to Sparta (240km), begged for help and was promptly refused. Back he ran to his commander on the fennel field.

It wasn't long before the Persians attacked. The Greeks, including Pheippides, fought with such brilliance that they won the battle, and the Persians turned tail and fled. Barely having drawn a breath, Pheippides hurtled off again to Athens to announce the joyful news. 'Rejoice, we conquer!' he wheezed, and promptly dropped down dead. The significance of the fennel field is that the ancient Greek for fennel is *maratho,* and the name of the battlefield was, of course, Marathon. Odd thought that now, every year, thousands of people run fennel fields all over the world.

Another place name celebrating swathes of wild fennel is Funchal, the capital of Madeira. Portuguese sailors stumbling on this unknown island in the Atlantic Ocean discovered a world of sweet feathery fronds and tall laurissilva trees, many of which have now disappeared. I have no doubt that fennel remains. The plant is native to the Mediterranean, so perhaps it had been carried here in the craw of a migratory bird, finding an ideal home despite the rough seas and the fierce winds.

I've been visiting the same village in the Touraine for five decades now and much has changed, but the fennel is just as I remember it from my childhood. It clings on for dear life, thrusting up on every bare patch of earth, right across the hillside. We use it occasionally, but the keenest customers are the gliding swallowtail butterflies with their long tails and wide wings. They lay their eggs here and then the larvae gorge on the leaves until they can eat no more. Emerging from their cocoons, the new butterflies keep themselves going through their brief month of life by sipping the nectar from the umbels of yellow flowers.

If you grow your own fennel, you'll know how lovely those flowers are, and how many insects enjoy them, humming and buzzing in a soporific drone in warm sunshine. It takes only a few weeks for the fruit of the plant to mature, a brace of seeds in each one, gently curving in embrace. As they dry, the two seeds separate to give us the familiar-looking spice.

Fennel seed is a renowned carminative. In other words it soothes a stomach bloated with wind. The 16th century herbalist, John Gerard, put it very nicely: 'Fennel seede drunke assuageth the paine of the stomache, and the wambling of the same, or desire to vomite, and breaketh winde.' Windy babies are given gripe water (which contains fennel) to soothe them, but windy grown-ups might well prefer a straightforward mug of fennel tea.

Notes on fennel

✪ The best fennel seed is probably going to be the one you harvest from your own fennel plants, wonderful used fresh or dried, but failing that the mantra is 'the greener the better'. Dull greyish seeds will be less fragrant.

✪ The most fashionable, trendiest spice on the market these days is fennel pollen. It has an intense, floral, warm fennel aroma and a ginormous price tag, generated by the laborious harvesting technique. One head of flowers provides just a teensy helping of pollen. However, it is genuinely wonderful stuff, and if you are really enterprising, you could grow and harvest your own. Once the fennel flowers are in bloom, cut the umbels off, tie them in a bunch upside down, safely encased in a paper bag. As the flowers dry the pollen falls off and is all yours. Dill pollen can be harvested in the same way. ➥

chicken & chorizo stew

Serves 4

8 chicken thighs

2 tablespoons extra virgin olive oil

1 large red onion, peeled and thinly sliced

250g soft cooking chorizo

4 garlic cloves, peeled and sliced

2 teaspoons fennel seeds

bouquet garni (1 bay leaf, 4 thyme sprigs,
  2 large parsley sprigs, tied with string)

400g tin chopped tomatoes

100g tomato purée

300ml water

salt and freshly ground black pepper

230g cooked butter beans

This is a luscious, big, filling stew based on a Spanish dish of chorizo and beans. Serve it with rice or lots of warm bread. If you use dried butter beans you will need roughly 150g: soak overnight, then simmer in fresh unsalted water until tender.

Pat the chicken thighs dry on kitchen paper. Heat the olive oil in a fairly deep frying pan, or flameproof casserole. Brown the thighs swiftly on all sides, then scoop out and set aside.

Fry the onion gently in the oil remaining in the pan until soft and translucent. Meanwhile, pull the skin off the chorizo and slice the sausage up roughly. Turn the heat up under the onions, and add the chorizo and garlic to the pan. Continue frying, breaking up the pieces of chorizo, until they are sizzling and crusty. Carefully spoon off as much of the fat as you can.

Return the chicken to the pan and add all the remaining ingredients except the butter beans, seasoning well with salt and pepper. Simmer gently for 30 minutes, stirring occasionally.

Add the butter beans to the pan and carry on cooking for a final 10 minutes. Taste and adjust the seasoning, remove and discard the bouquet garni, and serve.

Cooking with fennel seeds and pollen

Fennel is one of the most under-used spices. Not in Italy nor in Provence, but in many, many other countries. This is a shame, because fennel seed, in moderation, can transform so many relatively simple dishes, lifting them way out of the ordinary. A pinch of whole fennel seeds in a tomato sauce does wonders for it, and no one knows that better than Italian cooks. They love the sweet anise aroma and they know that it is a natural with pork, fish and tomatoes.

Fennel seeds find their way into Italian sausages (dried and fresh), succulent liver dishes, tomatoey pasta sauces, plates of curvaceous prawns and firm monkfish. Try slow-roasting duck with fennel seeds and vin santo or marsala and you'll see how the fennel scent and sweetness of the wine cut through the richness of the meat.

Fennel seeds are brilliant with many vegetables – in a potato salad, perhaps, or the dressing for roasted, skinned peppers, or tossed with steamed asparagus. I also love them with carrots, beetroot or orange-fleshed winter squash. Above all of these, however, the tomato undoubtedly has the greatest affinity with this spice – try scattering fennel seeds over halved tomatoes to be roasted to tenderness in the oven.

Fennel is not only a Mediterranean flavour. It is much used in Scandinavian baking, especially in rye bread, and it has taken a firm footing in the palettes of India and China. As well as being used in many curry blends, it is one of the spices in panch phoron (see page 213), the critical Bengali spice mix, and perhaps even more importantly, it makes up one fifth of Chinese five-spice powder (see page 211).

Fennel pollen is used in smaller amounts than fennel, but has a big wham of sweet, smooth flavour. It is resilient enough to be simmered or baked or seared, but is beautiful sprinkled over milky buffalo mozzarella or a fresh tomato bruschetta.

aromatic roast pork chops with orange gremolata

Serves 4

4 thick pork chops

1 garlic clove, halved

extra virgin olive oil, for brushing

salt and freshly ground black pepper

8 thyme sprigs

6 rosemary sprigs

4 bay leaves

1 tablespoon fennel seeds

Orange gremolata:

finely grated zest of 1 orange

2 tablespoons roughly chopped parsley

1 garlic clove, peeled and roughly
   chopped

I found this method for roasting pork chops in one of Elizabeth David's books many years ago, and still use it frequently. It depends on using great free-range pork and plenty of herbs and fennel seeds. I finish them with a sprinkling of gremolata – usually a blend of parsley, garlic and lemon zest, but here made with orange which works so well with both pork and fennel.

Preheat the oven to 170°C/Gas mark 3. Score the chops lightly on both sides, and make small cuts across the fat on the edges to prevent curling. Rub both sides of each chop with the cut garlic surface, then brush with olive oil and season lightly with salt and pepper.

Make a bed of the thyme, rosemary and bay leaves in an ovenproof dish just large enough to take the pork chops in a single layer, and scatter over the fennel seeds. Lay the pork chops on this aromatic bed.

Brown the pork chops lightly under the grill (unless the grill is in your oven, in which case, brown swiftly on a very hot griddle pan and return to the dish). Now cover with foil and bake in the oven for 40–45 minutes until the pork is cooked.

Meanwhile, for the gremolata, mix the orange zest, parsley and garlic together on a board, then chop together very finely.

Just before serving, pour off the excess fat from the chops and sprinkle with gremolata.

masala chai

Serves 3–4

8 green cardamom pods

1 teaspoon fennel seeds

4 cloves

1 cinnamon stick, snapped in two

8 black peppercorns

5mm piece fresh root ginger, roughly
   chopped

500ml water

1 tablespoon black tea (or 2 teabags)

500ml milk

2 tablespoons caster sugar

Masala chai is the spice lover's Horlicks: soothing, comforting and just that bit more interesting. No slippers and cardigan needed. The joy of it is that there are no absolutes. The masala, or spice blend, is as individual as the *chai wallah* who makes it. This is my current favourite, with a good dose of cardamom and fennel seeds.

Put all the dry spices into a mortar and use the pestle to bruise them lightly. Tip into a saucepan and add all the remaining ingredients. Bring gently to the boil, stirring once or twice. Simmer for 5 minutes, stirring occasionally.

Strain into glasses or mugs and drink swiftly.

There was bird flu and then there was swine flu and no doubt there are more flus to come. Who knows, there may even be one that lives up to its devastating reputation. If there is, then no doubt we will once again be faced with shortages of essential antiviral drugs. There's always something to worry about. I'd imagined that the last drug crisis was caused by lack of forethought, or lack of capacity at laboratories, or maybe lack of funds. These may all have played their part, but the real cause lay in the south-west of China.

star anise

The province of Guangxi and its neighbours Sichuan, Yunan and Guizhou, produce no less than 80% of the world's supply of star anise. Unexpectedly, it turns out that star anise is the best source of shikimic acid. From shikimic acid comes a chemical called oseltamivir, and this is the active ingredient in Tamiflu, the best-known weapon against the flu virus.

Several years of poor harvests followed by a severe drought in 2009 caused havoc in the star anise orchards of Guangxi. Yields were poor, the price of star anise zoomed up, and the makers of Tamiflu were faced with a shortage of the most important component in the drug. Now they are developing new ways of fermenting shikimic acid from E. Coli bacteria. So next time there's a major flu crisis, there ought to be plenty of drugs to go round.

Normally the climate of Guangxi and its neighbours is warm, steamy and rainy. Normally, it has an annual rainfall of 1250–1750mm, which is just what the star anise tree loves. South China is its native home, where it thrives (normally), though it is also grown in Vietnam and other Asian countries. It is a tall, slender evergreen tree, related to the magnolia, with pretty pale ivory or pink flowers. These blossoms appear amongst the glossy leaves twice a year and then it takes a lengthy 12 months for the extraordinary-looking fruit to ripen.

This starry fruit is made up of 8–12 carpels, fleshy boat-shaped coverings designed to protect the hard seed inside. It is picked when nearly ripe but still green, then sun-dried to the hard, dark brown flower of a spice. Almost all of the essential oil lies in the outer layer, but most of the shikimic acid is actually derived from the cushioned seeds.

I'm still trying to fathom what it is about the scent of star anise that makes it so different from other anise-scented spices, like fennel. And for that matter, why I love it so much when I loathe liquorice, though I suspect that's a matter of intensity. A mouthful of unadulterated pepper or cumin would be pretty unpleasant too. However, the former is trickier. Star anise is perhaps a little brasher, a little less sweet, a little merrier and a tad more seductive in a cheery, vibrant manner. One thing that is obvious, however, is its physical beauty. No other spice comes close in that department.

Notes on star anise

❂ Your average small glass spice jar was not built to house star anise, and yet the major spice brands insist on forcing them in. Result? Very few, if any, whole star anise flowers and lots of broken sections. Call me picky, but when I cook with star anise I want to see how handsome they look. It's the endearing characteristic of this particular spice. So, my advice is don't buy star anise from a supermarket. Take a trip to an Asian food store and take your chances there. You will inevitably have to buy a larger quantity than you could possibly need but the good news is that they last more or less for ever. What you don't cook with, you could add to pot pourri, or spray gold and dangle from the Christmas tree.

❂ Even in a roomier packet, there will be casualties. When you have to use individual separated segments, remember that there are usually eight of them in each star anise.

❂ I believe that you can buy ground star anise but I honestly can't see the point. It will have all the disadvantages of any ground spice, and will lack the visual appeal of the whole one. The exception to this is as Chinese five-spice powder, that invigorating blend of star anise, cinnamon or cassia, Sichuan pepper, ginger and fennel seeds. You could make your own (see page 211), but many of us will resort to ready made. Just remember to replace the half used five-spice powder when you next need it 6 months down the line. ❧

marbled eggs

Makes 6

6 large free-range eggs, at room
temperature

150ml soy sauce

3 star anise

2 tablespoons black tea or lapsang
souchong

1 teaspoon caster sugar

I adored making Chinese tea-marbled eggs with my mother when I was a child. It's a simple process, yielding the most glamorous hard-boiled eggs you can imagine. Make them for picnics or snacks, or serve as the focal point of a summer lunch. Using lapsang souchong gives them a divine smoky bacon scent.

Bring a pan of water to the boil and gently lower the eggs into it. Simmer for 9 minutes, then drain and run under the cold tap for a few minutes until cool enough to handle.

Gently tap each egg all over with the back of a teaspoon, or against the work surface, to crack the shell, without actually knocking it off.

Put the eggs, cracked shells and all, back in the pan with fresh water to cover and add all the remaining ingredients. Simmer quietly for 1 hour.

Turn off the heat and leave the eggs sitting in their tea bath for several hours. They can be transferred to the fridge once the liquid is cool. The longer they steep the better the spiderweb of markings will be.

Now peel off the shells to reveal the beautiful marbled eggs.

red cooked lamb

Serves 6

1.7kg shoulder of lamb

5cm piece fresh root ginger, peeled and
thinly sliced

4 garlic cloves, peeled and sliced

2 strips dried tangerine peel

1 cinnamon stick

2 star anise

4 tablespoons dark muscovado sugar

1 tablespoon rice vinegar or cider vinegar

6 tablespoons shaoxing wine (or dry
sherry)

5 tablespoons soy sauce

To serve:

3 pak choi, quartered lengthways

3 spring onions, trimmed and thinly sliced

handful of coriander leaves

Red cooking is a classic Chinese way of cooking meat, simmered gently in a broth flavoured with star anise, soy sauce, shaoxing wine and other aromatics. The cooked lamb can be eaten hot or cold, thinly sliced to make the most of it. I like it steaming hot with Chinese greens… so satisfying.

To serve the lamb cold, boil the cooking liquid hard to reduce by half, then cool. Arrange the lamb on a plate with batons of cucumber, spoon over a little reduced sauce and serve.

Put the lamb into a large heavy-based saucepan and cover with water. Bring up to the boil and simmer gently for 5 minutes. Take the lamb out and discard the liquid.

Rinse out the pan and return the lamb to it. Add all the remaining ingredients and pour on enough water to cover. Bring up to the boil again, then reduce the heat and simmer very gently for 2–2½ hours until the lamb is very, very tender, topping up the liquid level with more boiling water as needed to keep the lamb covered.

If not eating immediately, turn off the heat and leave the lamb to cool in the broth. Cover and transfer to the fridge. The next day, lift the congealed fat from the surface and discard.

Take out the lamb and slice thinly. Strain the broth and return to the pan. Bring up to the boil, add the pak choi and simmer for 2 minutes.

Divide between individual bowls, add the sliced lamb and top with spring onions and coriander leaves to serve.

Cooking with star anise

There's no need to do anything with this spice – no dry-frying or sautéing or pounding or grinding. All you do is put it in the pot with some liquid and whatever else you need. Simmer for however long it takes to cook the dish – 10 minutes, half an hour, 3 hours, all good. The fragrance of star anise soon permeates all. Lengthy cooking will neither increase the anise to unbearable concentration, nor diminish it to a whisper. The only thing you need to remember is that on average eight separated 'petals' make one star.

Star anise is a bit of a marvel with meat, especially in long, slow-cooked stews, where it blends with the rich savoury flavours that develop. There are many such braises in the Chinese repertoire, with sugar, wine and soy sauce working to create sublime concoctions. In Vietnam it is an essential flavouring in the stock for *pho*, the ubiquitous bowl of beef stock with noodles, meat and vegetables.

However, don't restrict star anise to oriental dishes. Slip a couple of stars into an old-fashioned oxtail stew, or a dark winy beef daube. Add it to the stockpot when making fish or chicken stock to use in a soup, or in gravy enlivened with a good slurp of port. I've even added star anise to the simmering mince for a cottage pie and it was delicious… essential, in this case, to fish out the pieces before topping with mashed potato.

It's not just a savoury spice either. Star anise is brilliant with fruit. To extract the flavour it must be simmered, so that takes us straight to the realm of fruit compotes. Try it with rhubarb (see right), apricots, cherries, apple and blackberry, plums or pears. When fresh fruit is scarcer in midwinter, simmer dried fruit with star anise, a cinnamon stick, a couple of glasses of cider and sugar to taste… lovely for pudding or for breakfast.

poached rhubarb with star anise & vanilla mascarpone

Serves 6

800g trimmed forced rhubarb

2 star anise

300g caster sugar

juice of 1 orange

Vanilla mascarpone:

250g mascarpone

1 teaspoon vanilla extract

1 tablespoon icing sugar

Call it poached rather than stewed rhubarb, add a flower or two of star anise and you have a glamorous grown-up pudding. Tender stalks are best cooked gently in a shallow layer in the oven, so they doesn't lose their shape. Vanilla mascarpone is lovely with it, but you could just as well spoon it over vanilla ice cream.

The fruit releases a copious amount of juice. Save some to make a rhubarb kir royale (dilute with sparkling white wine) or rhubarb fizz (mix with lemonade). Cheers!

Preheat the oven to 180°C/Gas mark 4. Cut the rhubarb into 3–4cm lengths, place in a shallow ovenproof dish with the star anise and sprinkle over the sugar. Pour in the orange juice, cover loosely with foil and bake for 40–50 minutes or until the rhubarb is tender, stirring once or twice. Leave to cool.

Beat the mascarpone with the vanilla extract and icing sugar. Pile into a bowl and serve with the rhubarb.

kalonji

poppy seed

nutty spices

Aka nigella, black onion seed, black cumin, black seed, gith, black caraway and charnushka... When the Prophet Mohammed told his wife Aisha, 'This nigella is healing for all diseases except As-sam,' she naturally asked what As-sam might be. 'Death,' he replied. Now that's quite a claim, but modern science is beginning to discover that it wasn't so far from the truth.

kalonji

These intensely coal black seeds are turning out to be remarkable. I've been cooking with them for some years now, but it was just a few months ago that I was introduced to their medicinal potential. In one of the many traditional herbal pharmacies that abound in the towns of Morocco, a member of staff grabbed a big pinch of kalonji seeds, folded them in a cloth and rubbed them hard. The pungent scent instantly cleared my congested nose. Later I discovered that the 14th century Islamic scientist scholar, Ibn al Qayyim recommended exactly the same practice. A case where sniffing at an antique herbal remedy makes consummate sense.

A cold, though, is pretty much incidental. More impressive are the discoveries that these inky seeds of *Nigella sativa* may have a role in combating everything from cancer and diabetes to asthma and hair loss, via a phenomenal number of other ailments. They, or rather the oil derived from them, can boost the immune system, too. All that eulogistic enthusiasm for kalonji inevitably throws up a few duds, too. It's highly unlikely, for instance, that 21st century research will ever prove Dioscorides' assertion that mixed with vinegar, kalonji becomes a first rate cure for dog or crocodile bites.

The plant originated in western Asia, but spread energetically across North Africa, and east towards India. It's a member of the buttercup family, but looks more like its cousin *Nigella damascena* – Love-in-a-Mist, the garden plant with pretty blue flowers surrounded by a lacey web of green. The two are not interchangeable, so don't try cooking with your garden flower-heads.

Kalonji's many pseudonyms appear to be designed purely to sow seeds of confusion amongst consumers. Nigella seems to be the most practical English name since it is unique to this spice, and directly connected to the definitive Latin name, but it is more frequently sold as kalonji (the hindi name) or black onion seed, which is plain wrong. Onion seeds look similar, but they don't taste the same and you won't get an onion if you plant kalonji seed. In much the same vein black cumin and black caraway are obviously misleading, while 'gith' is so obscurely old-fashioned that it can be ignored. In the States kalonji is sometimes sold under its Russian name charnushka.

Working out what you are buying is about as hard as it gets with kalonji. Using it is no problem. For cooking, for colds, even as a moth deterrent in amongst your jumpers, you can plough through a little jar in no time. With backers of the caliber of Mohammed and King Tut (he was buried with a jar of nigella seeds beside him) it has to have something going for it.

Cooking with kalonji seeds

Chew on an uncooked kalonji seed and you may not be overly impressed. A little bitter, a hint of oregano, a smatter of citrus. Once cooked, however, kalonji reveals a much more alluring character – nutty and delicious, but still retaining a herbal note in the background.

I love it mixed in with vegetables of all sorts and often add it to a dish of new potatoes (see right) or chunks of butternut squash that are about to be roasted in a hot oven. You might try it sprinkled over a spatchcocked chicken or salmon steaks before roasting.

It often appears on naan bread, or Arab breads, like a splattering of black ink, and is frequently included in Jewish rye bread doughs. The wonderful Polish Kolacz, a sort of yeast-raised cheesecake, may get a sprinkling as a finishing touch.

In India, particularly Bengal, kalonji is an important addition to curries, especially stirred – sizzling in hot oil – into dahls just before serving. And it is one of the five spices that make up Bengali panch phoron (see page 213).

My favourite brand of mango chutney comes flecked with black kalonji seeds, giving it a handsome appearance as well as adding to the flavour. I've taken a leaf out of their book, and now add it to relishes and chutneys of all kinds for exactly the same reasons.

roast potatoes with kalonji seeds & lemon

Serves 4–6

½ lemon, cut into 8 wedges

750g small new potatoes, halved if large

1 heaped teaspoon kalonji seeds

2 tablespoons extra virgin olive oil

salt and freshly ground black pepper

If you've not cooked with kalonji seeds before, then this is a good place to start. Toasted by the heat of the oven, they work very pleasingly with the bitter-sharp tang of the lemon to enhance tender roasted new potatoes.

Preheat the oven to 220°C/Gas mark 7. Cut each wedge of lemon into three. Put these and the potatoes into a shallow ovenproof dish and add the kalonji seeds, olive oil and some salt and pepper. Turn to coat the potatoes evenly in oil, crushing the lemon a little as you do. Roast for about 40 minutes, turning occasionally, until the potatoes are tender and browned. Serve hot or warm.

duck with moroccan tomato confit

Serves 2

2 duck breasts

salt and freshly ground black pepper

Tomato confit:

2 tablespoons olive oil

2 garlic cloves, peeled and finely chopped

2cm piece fresh root ginger, peeled and
    finely chopped

500g ripe red tomatoes, skinned,
    deseeded and roughly chopped

good pinch of salt

½ teaspoon ground cinnamon

½ teaspoon kalonji seeds

½ tablespoon orange flower water

1½ tablespoons honey

A recipe to try out when tomatoes are ripe and plentiful, this sweet-savoury tomato jam is intense and unusual. The kalonji seeds add texture and a mild aromatic nutty flavour. Although the jam is usually served as part of a collection of starters, it goes just as well with the meatiness of duck. The tomato confit can be made several days in advance. Serve it at room temperature or warmed through.

First make the confit. Heat the olive oil in a heavy-based saucepan and fry the garlic and ginger gently for a minute or so. Add the tomatoes, salt, cinnamon and kalonji seeds and cook over a low heat, stirring frequently, until the juices have almost all evaporated; this will take around 40 minutes.

Now stir in the orange flower water and honey and cook for another 10 minutes or so, until the mixture is so thick that you can mound it up in a heap. Scoop out into a dish and set aside.

Preheat the oven to 220°C/Gas mark 7. Prick the skin of the duck breasts all over with the tines of a fork. Heat a heavy-based ovenproof frying pan over a high heat. If it isn't non-stick, rub the surface with a little oil. Lay the duck breasts skin-side down in the pan and cook until golden brown underneath. Turn the duck over, quickly and carefully pour off excess fat, then put the pan in the oven. Cook for 7 minutes.

Take the duck breasts out of the pan, and leave to rest for 4–5 minutes in a warm place. Slice thinly and arrange on plates, on a bed of steamed green beans or spinach if you like. Spoon on some of the tomato jam and serve immediately.

The answer, before you ask, is 'No.' There is absolutely no danger that the Church Fête will be ruined when you discover the Vicar high as a dozy kite in the corner of the belfry, having consumed one too many slices of the very nice poppy-seed-speckled lemon drizzle cake. Not even if you feed him four slices of the Austro-Hungarian poppy seed pastry will he disgrace himself in an opium-induced trance. Sorry.

poppy seed

Having said that, he might still find himself in trouble should some random drugs-tester happen along, kit in hand. That's because the poppy seeds that we cook and eat come from exactly the same source as the laudanum of Coleridge's Kubla Khan and the less romantic heroin of modern drug dependency and all round grimness. Though they contain the teensiest trace of opiates they are not entirely exempt. So it is conceivable that a greedy vicar could test positive.

Papaver somniferum is the opium poppy, a plant with a beautiful flower and a chequered history. Quite where it emanates from is a matter of debate. Western Asia? Turkey? Or the western Mediterranean? Did it occur naturally? Was it a strange mutation of the ordinary scarlet field poppy? Or was it developed through human selection and cultivation?

What is more certain is that it has been used as a drug for millennia, by the ancient Sumerians, by Greeks and Romans and everyone who followed on from them. Its first mention in literature comes in the 8th century BC when the Greek author Hesiod mentions Mekone, the poppy town. From then on poppies make regular appearances in the great epics (The Argonauts, The Odyssey, The Iliad) and learned medical texts.

For better or for worse, the poppy is an extremely amiable and adaptable plant, so it thrives as happily in the mountains of Afghanistan as it does in your back garden. It takes around 110 days from sowing to harvesting of the seed capsule. Assuming you, or the farmer, are not after the milky opium, which is extracted from the capsule itself, the pod should be harvested when fully ripe and rattling. It will be turning brown, but needs to be picked before splitting open. It is then dried fully, crushed and the seeds exposed and cleaned, ready for sale.

Poppy straw is what's left over – the dried husk and the stalks – and is usually sent off to be processed for medicinal purposes. Curiously there's a bit of a buzz about a new cultivar of opium poppy called Norman. It's been developed in Tasmania, which is home to around 40% of the world's legal *Papaver somniferum*. Norman is as beautiful as his fellows, but is entirely free of morphine or codeine. Far from rendering him useless, he has been blessed with generous doses of thebaine and oripavine, potentially much stronger painkillers, with little risk of addiction.

Tasmania has succeeded in poppy cultivation where the UK has failed. Not for want of trying. In the late 18th and early 19th centuries the Society of Arts was all for encouraging farmers to cultivate drug crops in order to reduce medical costs. The opium poppy already grew wild in Norfolk and Cambridgeshire, so this didn't seem too tall an order. They offered a prize of 50 guineas or a gold medal to anyone who grew substantial amounts of opium. In 1797 John Ball of Williton in Somerset claimed the prize, and others followed on.

It was Mitcham, now in South London, which became the most successful poppy-growing area in the country. Here they specialised in producing dried poppy-heads rather than extracting opium (or seeds). Most of it was sent up to the markets of London, together with generous quantities of cannabis, another crop that Mitcham made its own. Far from turning Mitcham into a den of Victorian iniquity, the trade eventually died out. I notice that now, on Mitcham town's website they sing loud about the lavender fields that once surrounded the town, but not a whisper of those pretty poppy flowers.

Poppy seeds are very, very small. There are approximately 3,500 seeds in one gram. If you look at them very carefully, or better still under a microscope, you can see that they are not round, but kidney shaped. They also come in two colours. The European poppy seed is a slate-blue black, while in Asia, cooks prefer the white seed, which is really more of a pale ivory yellow.

stir-fried peppers with mozzarella

Serves 4 as a starter

3 assorted peppers (red, yellow, green or orange)

2 tablespoons extra virgin olive oil

2 garlic cloves, peeled and finely chopped

1 teaspoon poppy seeds

1 tablespoon drained capers in brine or vinegar

2 tablespoons roughly chopped parsley

salt and freshly ground black pepper

2 buffalo mozzarella, roughly ripped up

This dish of stir-fried peppers, speckled with poppy seeds and sharpened with capers, makes a brilliant quick starter with gobbets of soft milky mozzarella. Without the mozzarella, it can serve as a side dish – very good with grilled or griddled chicken, or a sturdy fish like tuna. Buy the smallest capers you can find.

Halve, core and deseed the peppers, then cut into strips. Heat the olive oil in a wok or a roomy frying pan over a high heat. Add the peppers and stir-fry for 3–4 minutes until patched with brown and semi-tender. Now add the garlic and poppy seeds and continue stir-frying for another minute.

Next tip in the capers and chopped parsley and toss through, keeping everything moving round the pan for a few more seconds. Season with salt and pepper to taste. Pile onto plates, adding the torn mozzarella, and serve.

Notes on poppy seed

✿ When you are looking to buy slate-blue poppy seeds you may do better to search the baking aisle of the supermarket than the spice racks, or better still to go to a Central European food shop or deli. For white poppy seeds you must go to an Asian shop, where they may be labelled *khuskhus* or *posto*, two of the many Asian names for them.

✿ For the majority of poppy seed recipes, you will need to grind the seeds to a soft pasty powder. Assuming that you don't have a poppy seed grinder (yes, they do exist), the easiest and most effective way is to use an electric spice/coffee grinder. For small amounts (a tablespoon or two), a pestle and mortar is fine. Many recipes suggest that you soak the poppy seeds first to soften them, then grind in a food processor. Frankly, unless you have a brilliant processor, this doesn't work well enough.

Cooking with poppy seed

Poppy seeds need to be cooked. Or rather they make more sense when they've been cooked. Raw poppy seeds are hard and taste of very little, and that's true for both white and black. So, fine to use as a decorative garnish of some sort – sprinkled onto a salad, or over devilled eggs, or the icing on a cake – but they will add little to the taste.

A spot of heat makes all the difference and it can be applied in a multitude of ways. In Europe there are several approaches. The simplest is to stir them into a cake batter (I always add them to a carrot cake) or bread dough, and/or sprinkle on top so that they will be cooked in a hot oven. The second, favoured in Central and Eastern Europe, is to grind them to a powder, and cook them with sugar and milk to make the most luscious filling for pastries, or dressing for sweet pasta dishes.

As a dressing for noodles or vegetables, fry them in plenty of butter (perhaps with a little chopped onion) then add the noodles or vegetables to the pan together with a little chopped parsley, or grated lemon zest or both, and toss to mix.

In India, where white poppy seeds are favoured over black, the approach is not the same. Poppy seeds are either stir-fried in hot oil with other spices or ground up and used as a thickener for curries.

spiced eggs with white poppy seeds

Serves 6–8

2 green jalapeño or Fresno chillies

1 onion, peeled

3 garlic cloves, peeled

1cm piece fresh root ginger, peeled

6 eggs, hard-boiled and shelled

2 tablespoons sunflower oil

½ teaspoon ground turmeric

1 teaspoon cumin seeds

50g white poppy seeds, ground

salt

1 tablespoon roughly chopped coriander

lime wedges, to serve

This earthy, satisfying Bengali dish of hard-boiled eggs coated in ground poppy seeds is known as *dim posto*. You can use the same method with potatoes or cauliflower florets instead of the eggs – just add a little more water and simmer, covered, for just long enough to cook the vegetables through.

Quarter the chillies lengthways and remove the seeds. Chop the onion, garlic and ginger. Make sure the eggs are dry. Heat the oil in a wok or high-sided frying pan. Add the eggs and fry briskly until patched with brown all over. Scoop out and drain on kitchen paper.

Now add the onion, garlic, ginger and chillies to the pan and fry until golden brown. Return the eggs to the pan, add the turmeric and cumin and fry for a minute or so, before adding the poppy seeds, some salt and 300ml water, at arm's length. Stir around, reduce the heat and cover. Simmer for 8–10 minutes. By now the poppy seeds should have absorbed more or less all the liquid to form a clingy, thick goo. Taste and adjust the seasoning.

Spoon into a serving dish and sprinkle with the chopped coriander. Serve with lime wedges and accompany with chapattis or naan breads.

poppy seed roll

Serves 12

350g strong white bread flour

150g plain flour

7g sachet easy-blend dried yeast

100g caster sugar

finely grated zest of 1 lemon

½ teaspoon salt

100g butter, melted

150ml soured cream

1 teaspoon vanilla extract

2 large eggs, beaten

Filling:

100g raisins

50ml rum

250g poppy seeds, ground

60g butter

150ml milk

80g caster sugar

2½ tablespoons honey

To glaze:

1 egg yolk, beaten with 2 teaspoons water

Variations of this divine poppy seed pastry are made throughout Germany and Central Europe, but the basic elements are the same: an enriched dough rolled up with a sweet, nutty poppy seed filling. The incredibly rich dough is a slow riser – make sure you leave it in a warm place, such as the airing cupboard, and allow plenty of time.

Mix the flours with the yeast, sugar, lemon zest and salt in a large bowl. Make a well in the centre and pour in the butter, soured cream, vanilla extract and beaten eggs. Mix to a soft dough. Turn onto a lightly floured surface and knead for about 10 minutes until smooth. Return to the bowl, cover with cling film and leave to rise in a warm place until doubled in bulk; this will take a good 2 hours or more.

For the filling, soak the raisins in the rum for an hour or so. Put the poppy seeds, butter, milk, sugar and honey into a pan. Simmer gently, stirring, for about 15 minutes until very thick. Stir in the raisins and rum, simmer for another 1–2 minutes, then allow to cool.

Preheat the oven to 180°C/Gas mark 4. Knock down the dough, then knead for a few minutes until smooth. Roll out on a well-floured surface to a 25 x 45cm rectangle – it will spring back again and again, but you'll get there in the end. Spread with the cooled filling, leaving a 2cm margin around the edge, then roll up tightly, to form a long plump sausage. Carefully lift onto a greased baking tray, laying it join side down. Cover loosely with a damp tea towel and leave to rise again in a warm place until just doubled in bulk.

Brush with the egg glaze and bake for 40 minutes or until the loaf sounds hollow when tapped firmly on the base. Cool on a wire rack. Serve in thick slices with a big steaming cup of coffee or tea.

cardamom

allspice

cinnamon

vanilla

cloves

nutmeg &
mace

warm, sweet & scented spices

Allspice is the Bob Marley of the spice world. Sure, it's been adopted here and there throughout the world, but it remains unquestionably *the* Jamaican spice. Its roots are literally and historically embedded in the islands of the Caribbean, though it is also found in parts of Central America. Jamaica, however, is to this day the most prolific producer of the spice, and uses it in its cooking with considerable verve.

allspice

When Colombus and his sailors found the 'West Indies' they fell upon the local spice with joy. Peppercorns! Super-sized fragrant peppercorns! Just what they were searching for. With visions of riches galore forming in their minds, they christened them pimento, after the Spanish for black pepper. How long was it, one wonders, before anyone noticed the error? Perhaps no one dared point it out, for the name stuck, and to this day pimento remains the Jamaican name for this spice. The British, of course, were far more logical and wise (biased, me?) and christened it allspice, because it does indeed carry hints of cloves, cinnamon, nutmeg, ginger and possibly, just possibly a nano-whiff of pepper.

The allspice tree (*Pimenta dioica*) looks a little like a bay tree, with sturdy, glossy leaves. In 1810 the writer Thomas Mortimer declared, 'It does not appear that in all the vegetable creation there is a tree of greater beauty than a young pimento… [the trunk] branches out on all sides, richly clothed with leaves of a deep green, which in the months of July and August, are beautifully relieved by an exuberance of white flowers. These leaves are equally fragrant with the fruit.'

It takes some 6–8 weeks for the clusters of fluffy ivory flowers to grow into clusters of firm green berries, which are swiftly harvested before they ripen fully and soften. Heaped up in piles, or secured in sacks, they are left to sweat for a day or two, then sun- or oven-dried before dispatch to packing lines, then on to you and me.

Using allspice

In Jamaica allspice finds its way into all kinds of foods and drinks but the most famous of all – full of fire and spice – is jerk pork. Jerk paste (see right) can be made at home and used not only on pork, but also on chicken and seafood and vegetables.

The original Arawak natives used allspice to help preserve meat as well as flavour it, and that custom has spread worldwide. In Scandinavia allspice is an essential element in pickled herring, whilst in the rest of Europe, particularly the UK, it regularly finds its way into blends of pickling spices. The unique multi-spiced flavour works wonders on everything, from pickled eggs to cucumbers.

The talents of this spice don't stop there. A spice as vibrantly aromatic as this has a natural place in puddings and cakes, in particular those sweetened with muscovado sugar. We're talking fruit cakes especially, but allspice is also a real winner in brownies or chocolate cake, or in a moist banana tea loaf. And I often use whole allspice berries in mulled wine or cider, where it imparts a warm festive scent that wafts cheerily through the house.

jerk paste

Probably Jamaica's most famous dish, jerk pork or chicken is a fabulous amalgam of high spice, high heat excitement. There are a thousand and one variants on the basic spice paste recipe, but they all have two things in common: allspice and chillies. This is a potent wet jerk rub, made with fresh searingly hot Scotch bonnet chillies, spring onions, and just enough soy sauce to smooth it out. Once made, jerk paste will keep in the fridge for up to a week.

Makes enough for 6–8 portions

2 tablespoons whole allspice berries

30g dark muscovado sugar

6 garlic cloves, peeled and roughly chopped

3 Scotch bonnet peppers, deseeded and roughly chopped

8 spring onions, trimmed and roughly chopped

1 tablespoon thyme leaves

2cm piece fresh root ginger, peeled and roughly chopped

1 teaspoon ground cinnamon

½ teaspoon ground nutmeg

2 teaspoons salt

1 tablespoon soy sauce

juice of 1 lime

1 tablespoon rapeseed or sunflower oil (optional)

Grind the allspice berries to a powder. Put into a food processor with all the remaining ingredients, omitting the oil if the jerk is for a fatty cut of meat, such as pork belly; put it in for chicken or fish. Process to a paste. If not using immediately, scrape into a jar, cover tightly and store in the fridge.

jerk pork

Serves 6

1kg piece pork belly

½ quantity jerk paste (see left)

The very best jerk pork is slow-cooked in a proper metal jerk drum or pit in glorious Caribbean sunshine. My back garden isn't ready for this, so I fall back on the oven, slow-roasting the pork to soften to a divine moist tenderness, electrified by the spices. Rub the paste in 24 hours in advance, so it has plenty of time to flavour the meat.

Using a very sharp knife (I use a Stanley knife), score the rind of the pork into diamonds. Turn the meat over and cut criss-cross patterns across the flesh, about 1cm deep. Rub the jerk paste all over the pork, making sure it gets right down into the cuts. Sit in an ovenproof dish, cover with cling film and leave to marinate for 24 hours, turning occasionally.

Preheat the oven to 180°C/Gas mark 4. Turn the pork skin side down and cover the dish with foil. Cook in the oven for 2½ hours, basting the meat every half an hour or so.

Now turn the setting up to 220°C/Gas mark 7. Uncover the meat, turn it skin side up, and return to the oven for a final 30 minutes to crisp up the skin.

Serve thickly sliced, with something plain and starchy to mop up the juices – rice, good bread, or even plain boiled potatoes.

cincinnati chilli

Serves 6

30g lard or 2 tablespoons sunflower oil

1 large onion, peeled and chopped

4 garlic cloves, peeled and finely chopped

1½ teaspoons ground allspice

1½ teaspoons ground cinnamon

2 teaspoons ground cumin

1 teaspoon cayenne pepper

1.5 litres water

1kg lean minced beef

1 teaspoon dried oregano

1 teaspoon salt

1½ tablespoons cocoa powder

400g tin chopped tomatoes

140g tin tomato purée

3 tablespoons Worcestershire sauce

2 tablespoons cider vinegar

Cincinnati is the self-styled Chilli Capital of the World, with more restaurants and cafés serving up chilli than anywhere else in the USA. Cincinnati chilli, however, is very different from the more familiar Texan chilli. For a start there are no beans in it, and secondly it contains a unique blend of spices, which includes both allspice and cinnamon. And it comes with its own all-important serving code (see below), and with 'oyster crackers', small hard savoury crackers, on the side.

For the home cook, two things should be pointed out. The first is that the mixture looks positively unattractive at the start of the simmering, and the second is that it really, really needs the full 3 hours of simmering to develop both taste and a more appealing appearance.

The chilli is usually served on spaghetti with a veritable thatch of grated Cheddar on top and that's known as three-way chilli.

Heat the lard or oil in a large heavy-based saucepan or flameproof casserole, add the onion and garlic and fry until tender and translucent. Add the spices and stir for a minute or so, then pour in the water and bring to the boil (it won't look good now, but don't worry).

Crumble in the beef, then add the oregano, salt, cocoa, chopped tomatoes, tomato purée, Worcestershire sauce and cider vinegar. Simmer the mixture gently for 3 hours, adding a little more hot water now and then if it gets too thick. You're aiming for an almost soupy consistency, runnier than that of a standard chilli or bolognaise. Stir it occasionally to make sure it doesn't stick to the base of the pan.

Serve one-, two-, three-, four-, or five-way.

One-way chilli A bowlful of chilli all on its own

Two-way chilli Spooned over spaghetti

Three-way chilli Served on spaghetti and then hidden by a major wig of grated Cheddar

Four-way chilli As for three-way, but with a scattering of chopped raw onions

Five-way chilli As for four-way, with a helping of kidney beans on top of everything else

banana ketchup

Makes about 900ml

120g tamarind block or 4 tablespoons
  prepared tamarind purée

5 ripe bananas

100g sultanas

1 onion, peeled and roughly chopped

2 garlic cloves, peeled and chopped

250ml cider vinegar or white wine vinegar

700ml water

150g light muscovado sugar

1½ teaspoons salt

½ teaspoon cayenne pepper

2 teaspoons ground allspice

1 teaspoon ground cinnamon

¼ teaspoon freshly grated nutmeg

½ teaspoon freshly ground black pepper

2 tablespoons dark rum

This is a well-travelled condiment. It began life in the Philippines and trotted around the world to the Caribbean. Apparently it was big during the war when tomatoes were scarce. It tastes something like barbecue sauce, something like a fruity chutney, but nothing like tomato ketchup. It's very good with cold ham or cheese.

If using tamarind block, break it up into chunks and place in a bowl. Cover with hot water and leave for 10 minutes to soften. Rub the liquid and pulp through a sieve and discard the fibrous residue.

Peel and thickly slice the bananas and mix with the sultanas, onion and garlic. In two batches, purée in a blender with the vinegar and some of the water.

Pour the banana mixture into a large, heavy-based pan, adding the tamarind, remaining water and the rest of the ingredients, except the rum. Bring to the boil, then turn the heat right down. Simmer the ketchup very gently for 1¼ hours, stirring fairly frequently to make sure it cooks evenly and doesn't catch on the base of the pan.

When the mixture is thick and mellow, draw the pan off the heat and stir in the rum. If you want to drive off the raw taste of alcohol, return to the heat for another 5 minutes. If you like the idea of a boozy relish, just leave as it is.

Either way, let it cool a little, then rub the mixture through a sieve, pressing through as much of the pulp as you can. Transfer to jars or bottles, seal and leave to cool. Store in the fridge, where it will keep for up to 6 weeks.

spiced double chocolate beer cake

Serves 10

300g plain chocolate, broken into pieces

250ml stout

200g unsalted butter, diced

250g caster sugar

2 large eggs

150ml soured cream

300g self-raising flour

1 teaspoon baking powder

1 teaspoon ground allspice

1 teaspoon ground cinnamon

¼ teaspoon ground cloves

good pinch of salt

White chocolate ganache:

300g white chocolate, broken into pieces

150ml double cream

In this cake all the stops are pulled out to emphasise the dark, rich chocolatiness of the crumb. As well as using the best plain chocolate (at least 70% cocoa solids, please), the addition of dark malty stout and warm allspice, cinnamon and cloves gives incredible depth of flavour. Softening the impact just enough is a rich white chocolate ganache.

Preheat the oven to 180°C/Gas mark 4. Base-line two 20cm round cake tins with baking parchment and grease the sides.

Put the chocolate into a medium bowl. In a saucepan, heat the beer with the butter until the butter has melted and the mixture is very hot, then pour onto the plain chocolate and stir until the chocolate has completely melted. Stir in the sugar. Leave to cool until tepid.

Meanwhile, in a large bowl, whisk the eggs with the soured cream until frothy. Mix the flour with the baking powder, spices and salt. Now beat a slurp of the chocolate beer into the eggs, followed by a big spoonful of the flour mixture, and then repeat and repeat until both are used up.

Divide the mixture between the tins, smooth gently and bake for 30 minutes until the cake springs back when lightly pressed in the centre, and the edges of the cake are just pulling away from the sides of the tin. Leave the cakes to cool in their tins for 10 minutes, then turn out and finish cooling on a wire rack.

For the ganache, chop the white chocolate pieces fairly finely in a food processor or with a large sharp knife and scrape into a bowl. Bring the cream up to the boil, then pour half of it over the chocolate, stirring constantly. After a minute, pour in the remaining cream and keep stirring until all the chocolate has melted. Pour about a third of the mixture into a separate bowl and as soon as it has cooled down place in the fridge. Leave the rest of the ganache to cool at room temperature.

Once the cakes are totally cool, sandwich them together with the thickened ganache from the fridge. Then use the other portion of ganache to ice the cake, spreading it smoothly over the top and down the sides. It's now ready to go.

Cardamom is the most perfumed and sensuous of all spices. It whispers of dusky maidens, mysterious boudoirs, languid heat, indolent comfort, seductive arts and exotic locations. Is it any wonder it appears frequently in the pages of the Arabian Nights? Or that it was said to grow in the Hanging Gardens of Babylon, built by King Nebuchadnezzar to assuage the homesickness of his beautiful young Persian bride?

cardamom

Cardamom's homeland, however, is far, far afield, in the Western Ghats of southern India. These steamy hills spread across the states of Tamil Nadu, Karnataka and Kerala and this is still where the vast majority of the world's cardamom is grown. Other countries, such as Sri Lanka and Guatemala, have taken up cardamom cultivation, encouraged no doubt by the fact that it is one of the world's most expensive spices, outranked only by saffron and vanilla.

Cardamom is closely related to ginger, throwing tall shoots upwards from a rhizome hidden underground. Strolling through a cardamom plantation is like walking through a bamboo forest that has been sprayed with warm perfume. The leafy cardamom fronds curve overhead, themselves shaded by tall trees to protect them from the belting heat of the sun. The strange part is the tangle of flowering stems that wriggle out from the base of the plants like Medusa's locks, sprawling across the earth. Technically these are known as panicles, bearers of the precious crop of cardamom pods.

Once the bright green pods have begun to set, they are harvested regularly over a period of months. The pods are carefully dried – either out in the sun, or in drying ovens – just hot enough to do the job, but not so hot that the scent of the spice is damaged. Good cardamom pods are green and crisp, oval in shape, but with a curious triangular cross-section.

As well as green cardamom pods, you may come across white and brown cardamom. The white have been bleached, which dampens the aroma, so are barely worth buying. Brown cardamom pods, sometimes sold as black cardamom, are bigger and rougher looking and are not in fact true cardamom pods at all. Although loosely related to green cardamom (they're both members of the ginger family) the taste is less subtle, more blunt and nowhere near as perfumed. Perfectly pleasant, but not in the same class at all.

Using cardamom

Much as you would expect, cardamom features elegantly and frequently in the cooking of India and Sri Lanka, where it is equally at home as a subtle fragrant note in a curry powder or paste blend as in a sweetmeat or creamy milk pudding. Favourites of mine are cones of the Indian cardamom ice cream, kulfi, and the richness of shrikand (see page 171). To give a gentle fragrance to plain rice or a pilaf or biriyani, I often throw 4 or 5 whole cardamom pods into the pan as it cooks.

Spice traders took cardamom from India right the way through the countries of the Middle East, lodging it firmly in their cuisines, echoing the dishes of its homeland and adding new ways of using cardamom to the repertoire. It makes a big impact in the syrup-soaked pastries of the region, and in the many milk puddings, but it seems odd to find it in the startlingly hot Yemeni relish zhug (see page 88) that is served at almost every meal. Cardamom coffee is simple but effective – a few slit pods of cardamom are pushed into the spout of the coffee pot so that the hot liquid flows out over them into the cup.

More surprising is the Scandinavian passion for cardamom in baking. I love the Finnish pulla, but Norway and Sweden both have a wealth of recipes for cardamom buns, breads, waffles and cakes. ➻

venison in the style of the mughal court

Serves 8–10

2.5–3kg boned, rolled haunch of venison

2 tablespoons cornflour

Marinade:

2 big pinches of saffron threads

2 tablespoons hot water

1 onion, peeled and roughly chopped

3 garlic cloves, peeled and roughly
  chopped

5cm piece fresh root ginger, peeled and
  roughly chopped

2 hot dried red chillies, broken into pieces

1½ teaspoons cumin seeds

1 teaspoon turmeric

1 tablespoon Mughal garam masala
  (see below)

90g seedless raisins

60g cashew nuts

3 tablespoons lime juice or lemon juice

1 tablespoon honey

2 teaspoons salt

150g Greek yoghurt

45g crème fraîche

Mughal garam masala:

10 green cardamom pods

½ teaspoon black peppercorns

1 teaspoon coriander seeds

1 teaspoon ground cinnamon

¼ teaspoon ground cloves

¼ teaspoon freshly grated nutmeg

If you have the slightest fondness for spices, then you can hardly fail to appreciate this legacy from the traditions of the royal Mughal kitchens. A big hunk of venison is marinated and pot-roasted in a paste of warm spices, blended with nuts, raisins and yoghurt, to produce elegantly spiced, very tender meat, bathed in copious amounts of fragrant gravy. It works well with a boned leg of lamb, too.

Serve it with simple pilau rice, gilded bright yellow with a touch of turmeric, dotted here and there with whole cardamom, and speckled with finely chopped coriander and pomegranate seeds if they are in season.

Begin by making the garam masala. Slit open the cardamom pods and extract the seeds. Put the seeds into a mortar or grinder with the black peppercorns and coriander seeds, and grind to a powder. Mix with the remaining spices. Store in an airtight jar.

Now for the marinade. Soak the saffron threads in the hot water for 30 minutes. Put all the remaining marinade ingredients, except the yoghurt and crème fraîche, into a food processor and process until evenly and pretty much smoothly chopped. Add the yoghurt, crème fraîche and saffron water and blend again.

Snip the string off the rolled haunch and open out flat. Spread 3 tablespoons of the marinade over the inside, then roll up again and tie as neatly as you can. Spread about a quarter of the remaining marinade over the base of a casserole dish, then lay the rolled haunch in it. Spoon the last of the marinade all over the outside of the haunch. Cover and leave to marinate for 24–48 hours in the fridge. Whenever you remember, turn the venison, and spoon the marinade back over it.

About 4 hours before you intend to eat the venison, take it out of the fridge and allow an hour for it to come back to room temperature.

Preheat the oven to 220°C/Gas mark 7. Cover the casserole with a double layer of greaseproof paper or foil and clamp the lid firmly on, to give a really tight seal. Cook in the oven for 1 hour, then reduce the heat to 140°C/Gas mark 1 and cook for a further 1½ hours.

Lift the meat out onto a warmed serving plate and leave in a warm place while you finish the sauce. Stir a few spoonfuls of the juices from the meat into the cornflour, to make a thin paste, then add a little more. Stir back into the juices in the casserole and bring up to the boil, still stirring. Simmer for 2 minutes, then taste and adjust the seasoning.

Slice the venison (you'll need a good sharp knife for this), and serve with the sauce.

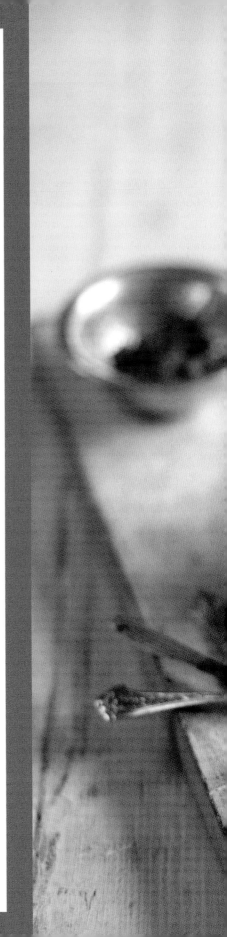

Notes on cardamom

✿ Always, always buy cardamom whole in its pod. Ready ground cardamom is phenomenally expensive, and the volatile oils that make it so delightful are genuinely extremely volatile. Within a remarkably short time of being ground they waft off into the ether, never to be found again.

✿ Although there are plenty of recipes where the pod is used whole, for instance for pilaus and other rice dishes, the real power lies in the seeds tucked up neatly inside. The only thing for it is to extract them, pod by pod. Take a small sharp knife and carefully slit open each one. Scrape out the little black or brown seeds that are clustered inside. This is the treasure. Grind the seeds in a mortar or an electric spice mill literally minutes before you use them to safeguard all of that fabulous perfume. It takes roughly 10–12 cardamom pods to yield up ½ teaspoon of seeds.

✿ You won't find black/brown cardamom on the shelves of your average supermarket or deli. If you want to try it out, you'll have to head off to your nearest Asian grocery store, where they'll probably be nestled amongst the other bags of spices. They are much cheaper than real cardamom, but no replacement. In the recipes in this book, use green cardamom every time to get the full scent.

shrikand

Serves 4–6

600g Greek-style yoghurt

generous pinch of saffron threads

2–3 tablespoons rosewater

10 cardamom pods

icing sugar, to taste

1 heaped tablespoon roughly chopped
    pistachio nuts

Shrikand is a pudding of divine fragrance, blending cardamom, rosewater and saffron in creamy strained yoghurt. Serve it on its own, or with slices of mango, or even with crisp thin biscuits to scoop it up.

Line a large sieve with a double layer of muslin. Spoon in the yoghurt, gather up the edges of the muslin and tie a knot to form a bag. Hang it up to drain over the sink or a bowl. Leave for 4–6 hours, until it is good and thick.

Scrape all the strained yoghurt into a bowl. Dry-fry the saffron threads in a small frying pan over a medium heat for a few seconds to crisp up, then cool and pound to a powder. Mix with the rosewater and let it stand for 10 minutes to dissolve.

Split open the cardamom pods, extract the seeds and crush them as finely as possible. Stir the rosewater and crushed cardamom into the yoghurt and sweeten with icing sugar to taste. Divide between 4–6 small bowls and scatter the pistachios over the top.

pulla

Makes 1 loaf

250ml milk

100g unsalted butter, diced

10 green cardamom pods

1 large egg

110g caster sugar

¼ teaspoon salt

7g sachet easy-blend dried yeast

600g strong white bread flour, plus extra
  for dusting

To glaze:

1 egg yolk, beaten with 1 teaspoon milk

granulated sugar, for sprinkling

My beautiful Finnish friend Enoma swears that her grandmother makes the best pulla in Finland. It's a soft, sweet bread, scented with cardamom – made for every special occasion in Finland and eaten at the slightest excuse, thickly sliced, with a cup of coffee. It features strongly at Christmas, of course, but is also baked for birthdays and anniversaries, family visits, and even to mark graduation ceremonies.

As this is an enriched dough, containing lots of butter and egg, you will need to allow plenty of time for it to rise in a warm place – an airing cupboard is often the best spot.

Put the milk and butter in a pan and heat until almost, but not quite, boiling. Leave to cool until tepid. Slit open the cardamom pods and extract the seeds. Throw out the husks and crush the seeds.

In a mixing bowl, beat the egg with the sugar and salt, then whisk in the tepid milk, yeast and cardamom. Beat in the flour in four batches, working the last batch in a little at a time until you have a soft dough that is barely sticky.

Turn the dough out onto a lightly floured surface and knead for a good 5–10 minutes, dusting with flour if necessary. Once it is smooth and elastic, return to the bowl, cover with cling film and leave in a warm place for 2–3 hours until doubled in bulk.

Punch the dough down, then knead again for a few minutes to smooth out. Divide into 4 pieces. Roll each one into a long thin roll, then pinch the strands together at one end. Plait the 4 strands together: starting at the same side each time, weave the outermost roll over and under the other strands to the other side. When you have finished, tuck the ends underneath and lay the plait on a lightly oiled baking tray. Cover with a dampened (and squeezed-out) tea towel, and leave again to rise for around 1½ hours until doubled in size. Preheat the oven to 180°C/Gas mark 4.

Bake the pulla for around 30–35 minutes until cooked through. To check, tap the bread on the base; if it sounds hollow then it is done. Quickly brush the bread with the egg glaze, sprinkle with sugar and return to the oven for 2 minutes. Transfer to a wire rack to cool.

I had high hopes of the Peradeniya Botanical Garden in Kandy, up in Sri Lanka's hill country. It's reputed to be a fascinating place, showcasing a plethora of exotic fruit and spice trees, not to mention a world famous orchid collection. My hopes were miserably washed away by the grey skies and ensuing torrential rain. On the speedy retreat to the café (excellent curry), I scratched the bark of the cinnamon tree, expecting a blast of sweet scented warmth. Nothing. Possibly because of the chilly damp, possibly the location – the best growing area is some 80 tortuously slow miles away, on the coast north of Colombo.

cinnamon

It may have been simply a matter of age. Left to their own devices *Cinnamomum verum* (also known as *Cinnamomum zeylanicum*) trees can grow as high as 20 metres, and this one was well on its way. It boasted a proper tree trunk, thick as a thigh, clad in an age-thickened corky bark. Cultivated cinnamon never gets that far, as it is regularly cut down to the ground, allowing fresh saplings to shoot up. After a few years they swell to the slender wrist-sized stems that give us cinnamon.

The plant is native to Sri Lanka, which still produces some four-fifths of the world's premium cinnamon. The rest comes from southern India, Brazil, Malaysia and the Caribbean, amongst others. Most of the cinnamon strippers and rollers in Sri Lanka are members of the Sakigama caste, and have learnt their trade from their parents and grandparents.

The process begins with the removal of the protective outer bark, exposing the tender cinnamon. The stripper scores through the flesh at the top and bottom of the stem, then makes cuts lengthways from tip to top. Carefully he eases off long rectangular strips of soft cinnamon. This is where the women step in. After a brief period of drying in the shade, the cinnamon strips are already curling in on themselves, but they still need to be rolled neatly by deft hands, and the inner cavities filled with slender shards of cinnamon, to give the ideal length (105cm) cinnamon sticks.

Cinnamomum aromaticum, or cassia, is closely related to cinnamon but is generally considered inferior, with a rougher, more bullish aroma. Not for nothing is it sometimes referred to as 'bastard cinnamon'. In the UK and many other countries it must be clearly differentiated from more expensive cinnamon. In America, however, no such restraints apply, and much of what is sold as cinnamon is actually cassia.

It is undoubtedly the true cinnamon that has been the prize over the centuries. The fate of Sri Lanka has long been buffeted by the blessings and curse of this native son. Everybody loves cinnamon but what should have been a brilliant trading commodity for Sri Lanka was, in many ways, its downfall.

First the Portuguese discovered Sri Lankan cinnamon, and in 1505, smashed their way into Sri Lankan history in order to get their hands on it. Next came the Dutch, some 130 years later, also lured by the sweet scent and the money it could earn them. They instituted the first organised cultivation of cinnamon, developing a system that has changed little over the centuries.

And finally it was the turn of the British in 1796, taking on this beautiful pearl of a country and with it the monopoly in cinnamon. Today you will find Da Silvas and Van Eycks and Grigsons in the phonebook alongside Wickremasinghe and Coomaraswamy, and that's largely due to cinnamon.

Using cinnamon

Everyone knows that cinnamon is fabulous in baking – in buns and cakes and biscuits and tarts. It is possible to overdo it, but you have to be extremely heavy-handed. I often find that the amount of cinnamon suggested in recipes is too meagre. Certainly if you are cooking from an American recipe outside the States it may be wise to increase the dose of cinnamon, to compensate for the milder nature of true cinnamon compared to American cinnamon.

Cinnamon has a natural affinity with dried fruit – typically in cakes and tarts – and with many fresh fruit. We love it with apples, especially tart baked apples with their fluffy flesh – mix a teaspoon of ground cinnamon with lightly salted butter, chopped dates and walnuts to stuff into the centre of the apples. Slide a cinnamon stick or two into the pan when stewing blackberries or pears, or even rhubarb. In Morocco and neighbouring countries, cinnamon is the finishing touch to a salad of sliced oranges that have been drizzled with honey; the perfect light revitalising end to a meal of rich ◆◆

winter squash salad with mint & cinnamon

Serves 4

500g chunk of winter squash, such as butternut or onion squash

3 tablespoons extra virgin olive oil

2 garlic cloves, peeled and chopped

handful of mint leaves

1 teaspoon ground cinnamon

2–3 teaspoons pomegranate molasses

salt and freshly ground black pepper

This is a great favourite of mine, inspired by Italian ways of cooking orange-fleshed winter squash, but given a North African flavour with the addition of cinnamon and pomegranate molasses. Serve it with baked ham and a peppery salad of watercress, or with cold roast chicken or turkey.

Peel, deseed and slice the squash thinly. Fry in two batches: heat half the olive oil in a wide frying pan over a brisk heat and fry half the squash slices evenly on both sides, turning them as they brown. When almost done, add one of the chopped garlic cloves to cook for a minute or two. Transfer to a shallow serving dish. Repeat to cook the second batch.

Set aside a few mint leaves for garnish. Chop the rest roughly and scatter over the squash while still warm. Sprinkle with the cinnamon, add the pomegranate molasses and season with salt and pepper to taste. Turn so that everything is evenly mixed, then leave to cool. Serve the salad at room temperature, with the remaining mint scattered over.

stifado

Serves 6–8

1.5kg chuck steak, or other good-quality
  stewing steak

4–6 tablespoons extra virgin olive oil

1kg small shallots, peeled

3 tablespoons red wine vinegar

150ml red wine

4 garlic cloves, peeled and chopped

2 bay leaves

3 cinnamon sticks

2 cloves

generous grating of nutmeg

3 tablespoons tomato purée

salt and freshly ground black pepper

This Greek beef, shallot and cinnamon stew shows how well cinnamon works to bring out the full, deep flavours of meat. The end result is a gorgeous rich stew, its various elements seamlessly blended by hours of slow cooking. Eat it with Greek orzo (pasta shaped like rice grains), or wedges of potato tossed in oil and salt and roasted slowly to tenderness.

Trim any sinew and excess fat from the meat, then cut into generous chunks, 5–7.5cm. Heat 2 tablespoons olive oil in a wide frying pan over a fairly high heat. Tip in the shallots and brown as evenly as you can, then scoop out and transfer to a flameproof casserole.

Add a little more oil to the frying pan. Pat about a third of the meat dry on kitchen paper, then add to the pan and brown in the oil. Scoop out and add to the onions. Repeat with the remaining meat.

Spoon out the excess fat from the pan, then return to the heat. Pour in the wine vinegar and wine, and bring up to the boil, scraping in all the brown residues on the base of the pan. Pour over the meat and shallots.

Add all the remaining ingredients and enough boiling water to just about cover the meat and shallots. Give everything a quick stir so that the tomato purée gets distributed around the pan. Cover tightly and either simmer over a gentle heat or cook in the oven, preheated to 150°C/Gas mark 2 for 2–3 hours, stirring once in a while.

If the stew is still a touch watery, take off the lid and leave to simmer for a while to reduce the sauce. Taste and adjust the seasoning before serving.

tagine or couscous. But don't imagine that cinnamon is allied solely to sweet dishes. It makes regular appearances in pickling mixtures and in chutneys (usually in stick form), and is surprisingly good with mushrooms. In much of the Middle East it is often used to flavour lamb.

In both the Lebanon and Mexico they drink cinnamon tea, scented and soothing. Simmer a pair of cinnamon sticks in 1 litre water for 5 minutes, then let it steep for another 2–3 minutes before straining into cups. Sweeten with sugar or honey if you wish. My favourite cinnamony drink, however, has to be Spanish hot chocolate. The best is as thick and rich as custard (it is similarly thickened with cornflour) and distinctly scented with cinnamon. Deliciously indulgent.

Notes on cinnamon

✿ Whole cinnamon sticks do not keep as well as other whole spices, since their protective outer layer of bark has been removed. Buy only three or four at a time and keep them in an airtight jar. When a recipe calls for a cinnamon stick it is generally implying a length of around 7.5–10cm.

✿ It is not easy to grind cinnamon sticks to a fine powder at home, unless you have an exceptionally good spice grinder. So buy ready-ground cinnamon for general use, and replace regularly (say every couple of months), to ensure that you are always using the best, most scented cinnamon.

✿ Studies have shown that cinnamon can have a positive effect on diabetes, but as with so many of these health claims, you would need to take it daily over a prolonged period of time for it to have any effect. The addition of a few spoonfuls of cinnamon to your apple pie does not make it health food.

rugelach

Makes 24

Pastry:

125g butter, softened

125g full-fat cream cheese

150g plain flour

Filling:

45g walnuts, chopped

30g raisins, chopped

60g light muscovado sugar

1 teaspoon ground cinnamon

To finish:

1 large egg, beaten

caster sugar, to sprinkle

These homely looking little pastries are incredibly delicious. Though they originated in Eastern Europe, I associate them with New York, where I first tasted them. There are numerous variations on the basic idea: triangles of rich, crumbly pastry rolled up around fillings of sugar and dried fruit and nuts and jam, and always, always a shake or more of cinnamon. This is one of the simplest versions, and the one I like best.

To make the pastry, beat the butter with the cream cheese until light and fluffy. Add the flour and beat in, but don't overwork – I usually resort to hands to finish the job. Once the dough is nicely mixed and smooth, wrap in cling film and chill in the fridge for 2 hours.

Preheat the oven to 200°C/Gas mark 6. Grease two baking trays. Mix the filling ingredients together. Divide the pastry in two; re-wrap one portion and return to the fridge.

Roll the other pastry portion out on a lightly floured board to a 22.5cm circle. Sprinkle half the walnut and raisin mixture evenly over the circle and press down lightly into the dough. Use a pizza cutter or pastry wheel to cut into 12 wedges. Carefully roll each wedge up, starting from the wide end, to form a sort of mini-croissant. Transfer to a baking tray, with the loose end tucked underneath. Repeat with the second portion of dough.

Brush the pastries with beaten egg and sprinkle with a little caster sugar. Bake for 12–15 minutes. Cool on a wire rack and eat warm or cold.

cinnamon toast

cinnamon

caster sugar

slices of bread

butter

My mum made cinnamon toast for me when I was a child, and I did the same for my children. It's nothing clever or fancy, just a simple treat that everyone appreciates.

Mix one part cinnamon to 4 parts sugar: 1 tablespoon cinnamon mixed with 4 tablespoons sugar will be enough for 3 or 4 slices of toast.

Toast the bread lightly on both sides, then butter generously. Dredge with cinnamon sugar and slide under the grill for a few minutes until bubbling. Cut into fingers and let it cool for a few minutes before eating.

On the tree they are pink and fleshy, slightly translucent and oddly alien. The change from fresh clove to dried clove is a veritable transformation from Little Miss Pretty-in-Pink to Dark Lady of Mystery. The original plump petite flash of pink is actually the flower bud of the clove tree. And if it were left on the tree as nature intended, it would turn into a dramatic flower with vivid scarlet stamen surrounded by four fleshy yellow petals. Beautiful, but rare.

cloves

The clove tree (*Syzygium aromaticum*, syn. *Eugenia caryophyllata* or *E.aromaticum*) originates in the Moluccas, once known as the Spice Islands. Lying at the eastern end of Indonesia, this chain of islands is still the world's major producer of cloves. Much of that production, however, is not destined for spice jars on kitchen shelves. No, a huge proportion is swallowed up by the Indonesian obsession for kretek cigarettes. Kretek means crackling, which aptly describes the sound of the cloves spitting and burning amongst the tobacco.

What doesn't go up in smoke is destined for the pot or for the pharmaceutical industry. Eugenol, or clove oil, is much used in dentistry. The vile pink or blue mouth rinse that sits by your elbow, as your mouth is plumbed and polished, may well have clove derivatives in it. That's because the clove has both antiseptic and anaesthetic properties. In fact, if you have a spot of toothache, then chewing a clove will help keep the pain at bay until you can get professional help. It's a trick that the ancient Egyptians cottoned onto around 3,000 years ago and it works just as well today.

It's a fair certainty that the Ancient Egyptians did not know that these same characteristics make eugenol ideal for anaesthetising pet fish before surgery. Surgery? Pet fish?? Mmm, you can get very attached to fish apparently and some of those ornamental koi carp are incredibly valuable... Sadly, if it all goes badly wrong, stronger doses of eugenol can be used to euthanise said fish. Aah...

At home, apart from the odd chewed clove in an emergency, it's probably best to keep cloves in the kitchen, where they rightly belong. Treat them with reverence. Over the centuries, many men have died for the sake of these odd little nails of a spice. Traded widely from time immemorial, cloves have been an incredibly valuable commodity. For the Moluccans this stroke of luck turned into a nightmare in the 16th century, when the Europeans' lust for spices drove them to war over the Spice Islands. Over ensuing years, the Portuguese, British and Dutch battled it out, decimating the local inhabitants with an appalling disregard for human life. In the end, the Dutch won out, and they held onto the Moluccas until 1950 when the islands became part of Indonesia.

Using cloves

In the 21st century, cloves have sunk to the back of the cupboard, a bit fusty, a bit old fogey, very old-fashioned. They're wheeled out of the old spices home for Christmas and the occasional Sunday outing – a shame, but perhaps unsurprising. Cloves are incredibly strong, especially ground cloves – even ¼ teaspoon too much can overwhelm all other flavours. The warm, resonant scent of cloves is a gorgeous thing, but needs to be handled with restraint.

Cloves have one huge advantage over other spices – their shape. I love seeing a clove-studded onion bobbing in a pan of milk destined for a béchamel or bread sauce, and it's a clever way to add a measured waft of cloviness to a sauce. The same trick works well in stocks, or even in beef or game stews. And a whole glazed and clove-studded ham is a spectacle. Although the cloves are largely decorative, they impart a lingering aroma to the fat of the ham.

I often add a couple of cloves to rice as it cooks. Again the aim is a subtle background flavour. They go into braised red cabbage, too, and take well, in strict moderation, to other sweetish vegetables, such as squash or parsnips. Cloves recur in innumerable spice mixes, rarely prominent players, but an essential base note. They find their way into curry powders, many garam masalas (see page 217), French quatre-épices (see page 210), Middle Eastern baharat and the very British mixed spice (see page 215).

Unlike the others in that list, mixed spice is very much aimed at sweet dishes and in particular, Christmas specialities, from figgy pudding to mince pies and of course, Christmas cake. On its own, those cloves find a familiar home in apple pie, but could happily move in with other fruits in pies and crumbles and tarts.

sri lankan chicken curry

Serves 4

2 tablespoons sunflower oil

10 curry leaves

2 medium onions, peeled and sliced

2.5cm piece fresh root ginger, peeled
and chopped

4 garlic cloves, peeled and chopped

2 green chillies, quartered lengthways,
seeds removed

7.5cm cinnamon stick

4 cardamom pods

3 cloves

3 tablespoons Sri Lankan roasted curry
powder (see page 214)

1 free-range or organic chicken, about
1.5kg, cut into 8 pieces

200ml water

2 tablespoons lime juice, red wine
vinegar or tamarind purée

salt

150ml thick coconut milk (see note)

This is a marvellous, intensely spicy curry from Sri Lanka, where their dark roasted curry powder is one of the mainstays in the kitchen. Sri Lankan curries tend to be hot, hot, hot, but I've reduced the chillies to give a heat that I can cope with comfortably. Serve it with rice and mango chutney.

Heat the oil in a large pan or wok and fry the curry leaves for a few seconds, then add the onions, ginger, garlic and chillies. Once they begin to colour, add the cinnamon stick, cardamom pods, cloves and curry powder and fry for another minute. Next add the chicken pieces and stir them around until fragrantly coated with the mixture.

Pour in the water, add the lime juice and season with salt. Bring up to a lazy simmer, then cover and cook gently for 30 minutes until the chicken is almost cooked through. Stir in the coconut milk and cook gently for a final 10 minutes. Check the seasoning and serve.

NOTE To obtain thick coconut milk, put the tin in the fridge for an hour or two before using. Open carefully, without jiggling it up and down. The thick coconut milk will have gathered at the top of the tin, so it can be scooped straight out into the curry when needed.

apple pie

Serves 6

Pastry:

220g plain flour, plus extra for dusting

pinch of salt

110g unsalted butter

squeeze of lemon juice

about 120ml cold water

60g lard, or more butter or vegetable
    shortening, diced

Filling:

juice of ½ lemon

700g cooking apples, or mixed cookers
    and eaters (about 6 medium apples)

3 or 4 cloves

90–120g vanilla sugar, plain caster sugar
    or light muscovado sugar, depending
    on the sweetness of the apples

15g butter

To glaze:

1 egg, lightly beaten with 1 tablespoon
    water

This is a really old-fashioned British apple pie, flavoured with a few whole cloves tucked in amongst the apples. If you don't like the idea of biting into a whole clove, use a pinch or two of ground cloves instead. Flaky pastry is the traditional pastry for a home-made pie like this, but if you don't have time to make it, then good-quality ready-made shortcrust is an acceptable alternative.

To make the pastry (allow plenty of time), sift the flour with the salt into a large bowl and rub in 45g of the butter. Add the lemon juice and enough cold water to mix to a soft, but not sticky dough. Knead briefly on a lightly floured board until smooth, then roll out into a rectangle, about 10 x 30cm. Dot the lard over two-thirds of the pastry, leaving the lower third, nearest you, stark naked. Fold this piece over to cover one third of the lard-dotted pastry, then flip the upper third, with its cargo of lard, over to cover the whole lot, as if you were folding a business letter. With the rolling pin, press down on the edges to seal them together neatly. Now turn the pastry 90° anti-clockwise, so that one of the sealed edges is nearest to you.

Roll the pastry out again to a 10 x 30cm rectangle, and repeat the dotting and folding process, using half the remaining butter. Seal the edges, give a quarter turn and repeat again. Repeat the rolling, folding and sealing a final time (without any fat, because you've used it all up). If at any time the pastry becomes sticky and over-soft with butter streaking through to the surface, wrap and chill it in the fridge for half an hour, before carrying on. Before using the pastry, it must be chilled for a good half an hour.

For the filling, pour the lemon juice into a bowl and half-fill with cold water. Peel, core and chop the apples roughly, adding them to the lemon water bowl as you do so (it will prevent them browning). Drain thoroughly, and pile into a 24–25cm circular pie plate, or other shallow ovenproof dish, mounding the apples up gently in the centre, and tucking the cloves in amongst them. Sprinkle with sugar to taste. Dot with slivers of butter.

Roll the pastry out on a floured surface. Cut a 1.5cm wide strip from two sides. Brush the rim of the pie plate with a little of the egg mixture. Lay the pastry strips on it, curving them round, and pressing the edges together. Brush with egg wash. Now roll the remaining pastry loosely round the rolling pin and unroll over the pie dish. Trim off the excess and crimp the edges together, pressing so that they adhere to one another and to the dish.

Cut out leaves or other decorative shapes from the trimmings and glue to the pie lid with a dab of egg wash. Make a hole in the centre for steam to escape. Chill for 15–30 minutes before baking, to minimise shrinkage. Preheat the oven to 180°C/Gas mark 4.

Brush the pastry with egg wash, then sprinkle with a little extra sugar. Bake for about 30–40 minutes, until the apples are tender and the pastry is golden brown. Eat hot or warm, with cream.

A glass half full of whole nutmegs sits on my kitchen shelf. They are all that remain of the bag of nutmegs I bought 6 years ago in St. Lucia and their aroma is still as true as the day I took them out of my suitcase. Now age has hardened them, but when I first grated my holiday nutmegs I was surprised by their softness. They must have been freshly cured, from that season's crop.

nutmeg & mace

The fruit of the nutmeg tree is a brilliant piece of packaging, a vegetal pass-the-parcel, with three layers to unwrap before winning the prize. About the size of the palm of your hand, the fleshy outer pulp is juicy, but tough and sour. It's not the kind of fruit you want to sink your teeth into, but it is used both in Indonesia and now in Grenada to make jams and jellies. Nutmeg fruit juice is tart and refreshing and for something more potent, Grenada's nutmeg fruit liqueurs are to be recommended.

Embedded in the centre of the fruit is the kernel, swaddled in a vivid red string vest. This is mace, a spice with a similar flavour to nutmeg, though perhaps a little sweeter and subtler. Under the mace is layer number three, a hard, brittle shell that protects the nutmeg itself, tucked up safely inside.

Nutmeg cultivation is a small-scale undertaking in St. Lucia, not the big deal it is in Grenada, 150 miles south. Until 2004, when Hurricane Ivan ripped across Grenada destroying lives and homes, nutmeg was the island's most important crop. The hurricane decimated 90% of the nutmeg plantations. The islanders are still in the process of rebuilding the nutmeg business, as they wait for new trees to mature and bear decent crops. At least now they know what they are doing. The first nutmeg saplings arrived on the island around 200 years ago, a totally new introduction to the island.

The nutmeg's natural home is the Moluccas, or Spice Islands as they became known when outsiders discovered the wondrous crops of both nutmeg and cloves that grew there. The Dutch, the Portuguese and the British fought tooth and nail for control of these exceptional dots of land wreathed in scented breezes afloat in the warm sapphire seas of Asia.

Greatest prize of all were the ten tiny Banda Islands, amongst them the mini island of Run, all of 3km long. Wisely, local merchants and Arab traders had kept the islands' whereabouts secret, so much easier in the days before satellites and mobile phones. But not foolproof. In 1512 the Portuguese found them, and soon the Dutch weighed in, with the British hot on their heels. Many violent encounters and vicious dirty tactics later, agreement ensued. In 1667 the British agreed to swap little Run for another almost inconsequential island on the other side of the globe – the island of Manhattan. Odd, isn't it, to think that if it weren't for nutmeg, New York would still be New Amsterdam, filled with Dutch-speaking Dutch-screeching yanks?

Unsurprisingly the Dutch guarded their nutmeg trees like they were the crown jewels. They didn't want anyone setting up a nutmeg business anywhere else, ever. A challenge if ever there was one, and eventually an enterprising adventurer weighed into the fray – the gloriously named Pierre Poivre, once a budding French missionary, now a full-blown, one-handed spice spy.

M. Poivre proved to be more adept at espionage and smuggling than he ever had been at converting the heathen masses. He got his nutmeg and clove trees and escaped alive, taking them to the Ile de France (Mauritius) and later to the Seychelles.

Liberated from its shackles, nutmeg now ambled round the world, eventually finding a propitious climate and terrain in the Caribbean. The great botanist Sir Joseph Banks, who travelled in the Beagle with Darwin, had a hand in introducing the spice to Grenada in the late 18th century, and the rest is history. When Grenada gained its independence in 1974, the new national flag featured a ripe nutmeg fruit, splitting open against a green background.

Every teenager seems to know that nutmeg is a hallucinogen, but parents shouldn't fear too much. To get a genuine buzz from it, you would have to consume at least half a grated nutmeg, probably more, and that would leave you feeling nauseous and ill enough to put you off trying again. Addiction is highly unlikely. ◆◆

bread sauce

Serves 6

1 small onion, stuck with 3 cloves

500ml full-cream milk

90g–125g fresh white breadcrumbs

freshly grated nutmeg or mace

salt and freshly ground white pepper

cayenne pepper

60g butter or 2 tablespoons double cream

A lone survivor from medieval feasts, bread sauce remains a brilliant, soothing accompaniment to roast chicken or turkey. To make it you must use the best white bread (not the cheap sliced stuff, which turns slimy), full-cream milk, cloves and lots of nutmeg. This is my mother's recipe, from her book *English Food*, and it's the one I've used since I was a child helping to make Sunday lunch.

Put the onion and milk into a basin and bring it to just below boiling point – this can be done over a pan of simmering water or in a slow oven. The point is to infuse the milk with the flavour of onion and cloves, so the longer the milk takes to come to boiling point the better.

Remove the onion and whisk in the breadcrumbs until the sauce is thick, with all the milk taken up. Keep the basin over the boiling water until the sauce is heated through. If it seems on the thin side – bread sauce should not spread very much when put on to a plate – add more crumbs. If it seems so firm that a spoon stands up in it, add a little more milk.

Season with nutmeg or mace, with salt and with the peppers. Finally stir in the butter or cream and spoon into a serving bowl. Sprinkle with a tiny flutter of cayenne and serve.

Notes on nutmeg and mace

✪ There is no point, absolutely no point, in buying ground nutmeg. Its power evaporates in a jiffy. Grating your own is easy enough if you have a nutmeg grater (a small fine-toothed grater) or a fine microplane grater. Whole nutmegs last indefinitely.

✪ If you happen to be travelling in nutmeg-growing lands, and come across whole nutmeg kernels for sale, buy plenty. Carefully break the mace off the outsides and store in an airtight jar. You'll hear the nutmeg proper rattling in its shell, which cracks open easily (use a nutcracker, or tap with a rolling pin) when you need the nutmeg.

✪ Mace is nearly always used whole, so when buying look for larger blades of the spice, rather than tiny dusty shards.

Using nutmeg and mace

Although you can grind up mace, it seems a shame to destroy its unusual lacy form. So, save mace for use in pickles and chutneys and infusions – for milk or mulled wine, for instance – or tie up in a bouquet garni with herbs to use in a soup or stew. The occasional recipe calls for ground mace, but nutmeg is an acceptable substitution. Though not identical, the flavours are very similar.

Nutmeg is a wonderful spice that has embedded itself firmly in Western cuisine. I can't imagine mashed potatoes without a good scrape of nutmeg stirred in just before serving, and who would want a custard tart if it didn't come complete with lashings of nutmeg? It is utterly at home in milk and custard-based dishes of so many kinds, from a simple white sauce to a slow-baked rice pudding.

Nutmeg and cheese, be it goat's or cow's or sheep's, is usually a brilliant combination – try grating nutmeg over a cheese omelette, or cheese on toast. It is also a joy with a number of vegetables. Spinach is the obvious partner, but I like nutmeg stirred into a squash or sweet potato purée, or included in the white sauce for cauliflower cheese. Or jazz up lightly cooked courgettes or carrots with a knob of butter and a flattering dash of nutmeg.

In India, nutmeg is used in many spiced recipes, from biriyanis to bhuna gosht, and often appears in garam masala blends (see page 217). Inevitably, it features a great deal in Indonesian dishes, some of which have connections to the Dutch era – kue kering biscuits, for instance, are a rich buttery confection, laced amply with sweet, fragrant nutmeg.

low-rise goat's cheese & spinach soufflé

Serves 4

60g unsalted butter, plus extra for greasing

450g spinach, tough stalks removed

1 onion, peeled and chopped

45g plain flour

150ml milk

300g goat's cheese, derinded and crumbled

4 large eggs, separated, plus an extra egg white

juice of ½ lemon

½ nutmeg, grated

salt and freshly ground black pepper

sprinkling of freshly grated Parmesan (optional, but good)

Weird, isn't it, how items just disappear when you move house? My round, deep soufflé dish is nowhere to be found. So now I've taken to making low-rise soufflés in shallower gratin dishes and we all love them. More of the brown top, a little quicker to cook and even if they don't look quite so impressive, there's no anxiety involved. This nutmeg-spiced spinach and goat's cheese low-rise is something of a favourite.

Preheat the oven to 220°C/Gas mark 7. Grease a shallow 25x18cm (or thereabouts) ovenproof dish with a little butter. Rinse the spinach and shake off excess water.

In a large saucepan, fry the onion gently in the butter, until tender and translucent. Now add the spinach, packing it in tightly, clamp on the lid and cook for 4 minutes. Stir, cover again and cook for another 10 minutes until the spinach is very soft. Sprinkle over the flour and stir in. Now gradually stir in the milk. Simmer for another 10 minutes, stirring frequently until very thick.

Take off the heat and stir in the goat's cheese, breaking it up into smaller knobbles with the spoon. Next stir in the egg yolks, one at a time, followed by the lemon juice. Season with nutmeg, salt and pepper, making the seasoning a tad larger than life, as it will be softened by the egg whites.

In a separate bowl, whisk the 5 egg whites until they form stiff peaks. Beat 1 tablespoon into the spinach mixture to loosen it, then fold in the remainder.

Scrape the mixture into the prepared dish and sprinkle with the Parmesan, if using. Bake for 25 minutes, until puffed and browned, but still with a teensy wobble when tapped. Serve instantly.

custard tart

Serves 8

Pastry:

120g unsalted butter

200g plain flour, plus extra for dusting

2 tablespoons icing sugar

finely grated zest of 1 orange

pinch of salt

1 large egg

1 tablespoon orange juice

Filling:

600ml double cream

100ml milk

3 large eggs, plus 3 large egg yolks

75g vanilla sugar (or caster sugar, plus
½ teaspoon vanilla extract)

1 whole nutmeg, freshly grated

A British custard tart is distinguished by its copious helping of nutmeg, and I just love it. In this version there is a hint of orange in the pastry, but otherwise it is much as everyone's granny would have made it. Simple. Classic. Good.

To make the pastry, put the butter, flour, icing sugar, orange zest and salt into a food processor and pulse together until the mixture forms crumbs. Add the egg and orange juice and process again until it forms a sticky ball. Scrape all the dough out onto a sheet of cling film. Dust your hands with flour and form the dough into a ball, then pat down to make a thick disc. Wrap in cling film and chill in the fridge for at least an hour.

Roll the dough out thinly on a lightly floured surface and use to line a 22cm tart tin with removable base. Leave the excess overhanging over the rim. Chill for at least 30 minutes.

Preheat the oven to 180°C/Gas mark 4 and put a baking sheet inside to heat up. Prick the base of the pastry all over with a fork. Line the case with a double layer of cling film and fill with baking beans. Slide straight onto the hot baking tray in the oven and bake for 12–15 minutes to set the pastry. Lift out the cling film and beans. With a sharp knife, trim off the pastry overhanging the edge of the tart tin, then return the pastry case to the oven for 10 minutes to dry out.

For the filling, slowly bring the cream and milk up to the boil. Meanwhile, whisk the eggs, egg yolks and sugar together in a large bowl. Slowly pour on the hot cream mixture, whisking constantly, then whisk in two-thirds of the nutmeg. Transfer to a jug.

Open the oven door and slide the pastry case halfway in. Pour the filling into the case (it should be filled to the brim), then carefully slide it right into the oven and close the door. Bake for around 25–30 minutes until just set but still with a slight wobble in the centre. Grate the remaining nutmeg over the top and serve warm or cold.

grenada rum punch

In Grenada they use a set formula for making rum punch and it goes just like this:

one of sour

two of sweet

three of strong

four of weak

In other words, mix together one part lime juice (sour) and two parts sugar syrup (equal volumes of sugar and water boiled together for a couple of minutes, then cooled). Add three parts good, strong rum and dilute the lot with four parts water. That's not quite all, though. To finish the drink, add a few drops of Angostura bitters, and grate plenty of fresh nutmeg over the top. Cheers!

Hijacked by its own success, gorgeous vanilla has lost its glamour. Plain, safe, pleasant, but so commonplace that it has taken on new meaning in modern parlance: it whispers 'safe, unadventurous'. Who but a wimp would settle for a vanilla warrant (a financial warrant with standard terms and no special clauses) or vanilla sex (probably the missionary position)?

vanilla

Vanilla ice cream has become the default setting, a standard so harmless and unchallenging that only dullards and children bother with it. And it's all because vanilla has invaded our lives – vanilla cakes and creams, vanilla biscuits, custards and milkshakes, vanilla-scented hand cream and shower gel, face creams and toilet freshener, vanilla absolutely everywhere. Or is it? Well no, of course not. Not the real thing, not the genuine exotic, sensuous, highly desirable spice that sends shivers of delight over the tongue. Genuine vanilla is a comparatively expensive commodity, its price held high by the need for dedicated labour amongst the vanilla vines. Most of the vanilla flavouring ladled into the ocean of vanilla products crowding around us has never, ever, come close to a vanilla plant, since much of it is derived from wood.

The vanilla orchid is the only orchid that yields an edible fruit. Native to Mexico, it is a climbing plant, with an unremarkable green and white flower. The Totonaco Indians were the first to spot its potential. This is their story of the origin of vanilla:

Long ago one of the wives of their King, Teniztli, gave birth to a daughter of such inspiring beauty that they named her Morningstar. They immediately promised her to the god Tonacayohua, and she was dispatched to his temple high up in the mountains. A vow of chastity was part of the deal, not that she had any choice about it.

Fifteen years later she was glimpsed by a handsome prince who fell head-over-heels in love with her. Xzakan-oxga (Young Deer) kidnapped his princess, who instantly fell for him. As they raced through the rain forest, they were confronted by a fire-breathing monster. They ran away straight into the arms of the even more terrifying priests who promptly beheaded them both. Where their blood mingled on the ground, grew a climbing orchid with perfumed flowers – the vanilla vine. How deliciously romantic.

When the Aztecs conquered the Totonaco, they came up with the idea of marrying chocolate and vanilla together in a drink. Then along came the Spaniards, who appropriated lands, gold, silver and both chocolate and vanilla. Well, who wouldn't?

The trouble with the mousy little vanilla orchid, however, is that its flowers are notoriously difficult to pollinate. There's one insect and one insect only that does it. Unfortunately the tiny melipona bee is a seriously stay-at-home bug who hates foreign travel. So, although vanilla would grow in other tropical countries, it wouldn't produce the precious pods.

Then in 1841 a 12-year-old slave named Edmond Albius living on Ile Bourbon (now Réunion) had a brainwave, working out how to pollinate the short-lived flowers by hand. From then on it was all systems go. To this day Réunion and Madagascar still produce what are considered the finest vanilla pods of all.

Even now every single vanilla flower has to be pollinated by hand in order to produce a pod and that's just the start of the process. The freshly harvested pods demand 3–6 months of curing, which involves killing and sweating amongst other strange processes, in order to develop the full, deep, thrilling scent of true vanilla.

Varieties of vanilla

There are three principal vanilla varieties. The most widely grown and still the king is Madagascar or Bourbon *Vanilla planifolia*, from the islands of Madagascar, Réunion, Comoros and Seychelles. Then there is *Vanilla tahitiensis*, grown in French Polynesia, which has a milder, but fruitier flavour. And finally there's Mexican vanilla, again *Vanilla planifolia*, but grown in its land of origin. Although less powerful than Bourbon, it can have a wonderfully complex flavour.

red onion & vanilla soup

Serves 4

750g red onions, peeled and thinly sliced

2 tablespoons extra virgin olive oil

1 vanilla pod

1 heaped teaspoon coriander seeds,
  crushed

1 heaped tablespoon pudding rice

750ml chicken stock

salt and freshly ground black pepper

To serve:

a little single or whipping cream (optional)

a little chopped parsley

Oh my, what a revelation! This was my breakthrough savoury vanilla recipe and I just love it. So simple and so good. And a dramatic lilac slate colour, as a bonus. What more do you want? Be generous with both salt and pepper to bring out the best in this soup.

Put the onions and olive oil in a large saucepan together with the vanilla pod and crushed coriander seeds. Stir, then cover tightly and leave to sweat and cook down over a low heat for 40–45 minutes, stirring once in a while.

When the onions are beautifully soft, stir in the rice and then the stock. Season generously with salt and pepper. Bring up to the boil and simmer for around 15 minutes until the rice is soft. Remove the vanilla pod, and then purée the soup using a blender.

Taste and adjust the seasoning, then reheat the soup if necessary. Serve topped with a drizzle of cream, if you like, and a sprinkling of chopped parsley.

Vanilla in savoury dishes

Vanilla is a sweet spice that leaps to life in the presence of sugar and for years I've avoided too-clever concoctions of vanilla and seafood or meat. But now I've been forced to reconsider and even to relent. Vanilla can be a positively appealing flavour in soups made with some of the sweeter vegetables such as winter squash or onions or even sweetcorn, but for something more subtle that you won't have to explain away to your guests, try adding a teaspoonful of extract to a tomato sauce when it is nearly cooked. It should be unobtrusive, but it will definitely heighten the flavour of the tomatoes.

With seafood, you need to err on the side of caution, but again delicate use of vanilla can release more of the natural taste. More robust flesh – chicken or guinea fowl, or even red meat – can take a stronger shot, but don't get carried away.

How to buy vanilla

Vanilla comes in many forms and from many places. Traditionally Madagascar or Bourbon vanilla was considered to be the very best, but things are changing. Recently I've bought Ugandan vanilla that is every bit as good if not better. None of these are cheap options, but they are totally worth paying for.

Every cook's kitchen should find room for at least two forms of vanilla: the pods and either extract or paste. If you have an old, dusty (I hope) bottle of vanilla flavouring or vanilla essence with the words 'vanillin' or 'flavouring' semi-hidden in small type, turf it out.

Vanilla pods These are the purest, most natural form of vanilla, though not always the easiest to use. The best pods are plump, sleek, supple and softly glossy, a deep, dark mahogany brown and charismatically scented. A dusting of white vanillin crystals on the outside is not necessarily an indication of extra potency, but nor is it a bad thing either. A split at one end, on the other hand, is a sign that the vanilla pod was fully ripened on the vine and should therefore have a really full vanilla flavour.

Although the price seems extortionate, remember that each pod can be used 2, 3 even 4 times, if you take care of it. After each use, rinse the pod gently in warm water, dry and store in a jar of caster sugar (see vanilla sugar, page 202). If you build up a collection of pods, then bury one or two of them in a jar of pudding rice as well, ready to turn into a creamy rice pudding at the drop of a hat. ➥

vanilla chicken with peppers & white wine

Serves 4

1 free-range or organic chicken, about 1.5kg, jointed into 8 pieces

3 red or yellow peppers

1 tablespoon extra virgin olive oil

100ml dry white wine

few thyme sprigs

Spice rub:

½ teaspoon vanilla bean paste, or the seeds from 1 vanilla pod and ¼ teaspoon vanilla extract

½ teaspoon coarse sea salt

½ teaspoon thyme leaves

finely grated zest of 1 lemon

¼ teaspoon freshly ground black pepper

1 tablespoon extra virgin olive oil

The scent of vanilla wafts through this dish quietly, but with assurance. I doubt that many will guess the mystery ingredient, but they will love the taste anyway, and that's what counts.

For the spice rub, just mix all the ingredients together in a large bowl. Add the chicken pieces and turn them in the mixture, massaging it all over them. Cover and leave to marinate for at least 1 hour, but far better a full 24 hours.

Preheat the oven to 220°C/Gas mark 7. Halve, core and deseed the peppers, then cut into broad strips. Put the peppers and olive oil in a roasting tin or shallow ovenproof dish with a little salt (not too much as some will leach off the chicken), and turn to coat the peppers lightly in oil.

Add the chicken to the tin, distributing the pieces amongst the peppers. Pour over the wine and scatter over the thyme sprigs. Roast for 45 minutes or so, turning over pieces and stirring around twice, until the chicken is cooked through. Check the seasoning.

Serve with rice.

For a comparatively mild blessing of vanilla use the pod whole, just as it comes. To develop more impact, slit it in half lengthways so that more of the inner scent is released. For maximum charge, go one step further by scraping out the tiny sticky black seeds in the heart of the slit pod, and then stirring them into the mixture together with the still surprisingly potent pod.

Vanilla pods release their scent most easily and readily in hot wet solutions. In other words, simmered or infused in syrups, milk, cream or other liquids. This is precisely what's called for when making custards, jellies, poached fruit, milk puddings, sauces, soups and so on. Add the pod to the pan with the cold liquid and bring up to the boil gently, then keep it hot, but just off the boil for a good 15 minutes or longer, time permitting.

Vanilla extract The best kind of vanilla extract is made by macerating lengths of vanilla pod in alcohol for 3 months or longer. The result is a dark, powerful vanilla liquid that begs to be incorporated into cakes, biscuits and puddings of all kinds. It keeps for (almost) ever, as long as it is in a dark bottle and stored away from light. Great stuff. In America legal definitions ensure the intensity and quality of extract. Regulation disappears elsewhere, so check labels carefully, and if there is a mention of vanillin or other synthetic additives, steer clear.

Vanilla paste Literally puréed vanilla pod moistened with just enough vanilla extract to render it usable, good vanilla paste will bring the ultimate all-round shouting and dancing vanilla show to your cooking. Tread a little cautiously at first until you've got the measure of it, then embrace the full grandeur of the flavour. As with the extract, keep in a dark jar, away from sunlight.

Vanilla sugar This is simply sugar that has naturally absorbed the scent from a vanilla pod and can be made at home with no effort. Store 1 or 2 vanilla pods (or more) in an airtight jar of sugar. After a week or so, it will have been transformed into vanilla sugar. Every time you use the scented sugar, top the jar up with more sugar to keep the supply going. Every time you use the pod, just rinse, dry and return to the jar.

For a stronger version, put sugar and roughly chopped vanilla pod in a processor and whiz to a powder. Use when you want a blast of vanilla rather than a restrained backdrop. ➥

poached cherries with vanilla & rosé

Serves 3–4

500g cherries

1 vanilla pod, slit open lengthways

3 strips of orange zest

juice of 1 orange

125g caster sugar

200ml rosé or dry white wine

Cherries are quite possibly my favourite fruit and I particularly like this way of using them. The vanilla-infused cherries bob merrily in the scented syrup, just begging to be spooned over ice cream or Greek-style yoghurt, or perhaps a baked custard, or cream cheese whipped with a little cream, or rice pudding, or morning cereal (the alcohol will have cooked out), or a slice of moist polenta cake or rich chocolate cake.

Remove the stalks from the cherries. If you want to stone them, go right ahead, doing it over a bowl to catch the juice. To be honest, I don't bother. Put all the ingredients into a medium saucepan and stir over a medium heat until the sugar has dissolved. Bring up to a lazy simmer and simmer very quietly for 10 minutes.

Leave to cool, then remove the orange zest and vanilla pod (wash and store the pod). Serve the cherries and their juices spooned over whatever seems right and pleasing to you.

NOTE In the autumn, use the same recipe for poaching peeled, cored and thickly sliced pears; use red wine instead of rosé, and simmer for 20–30 minutes until the pears are translucent. And then later on, in the dark of winter, use prunes instead of pears, again with red wine, simmering for around 15 minutes.

Vanilla essence Trying to work out what vanilla essence actually means is a bit of a nightmare. Some of it is made from synthetic vanillin (and must say this on the label), whilst other brands may well contain some genuine vanilla. Heat extraction and chemical extraction methods may or may not have been used. So, my advice is to leave it well alone. Spend a little more on a reputable brand of vanilla extract or vanilla paste.

Vanilla flavouring/vanillin You really don't want this. Cheap it may be but that's because it lacks one all-important ingredient – genuine vanilla. Flavouring is a synthetic concoction, quite possibly extracted from wood shavings. Yup, there's vanillin in wood, believe it or not, but it's not the classy multi-faceted, complex kind of scent that you get from a real vanilla pod. This is crude, slightly bitter and rough. Best avoided.

Home-made vanilla extract One day, it may just happen that you find yourself burdened with a surfeit of vanilla pods, in which case try making your own vanilla extract as follows: Take 10 vanilla pods, slit them open lengthways and scrape out the seeds. Chop the pods into 2cm long pieces. Put the pods and seeds into a clean bottle or kilner jar and cover with 300ml vodka. Seal tightly and shake, then hide in a dark cupboard. Shake again every 2 or 3 days for 2 weeks, then forget about it for 4 months. By this time your vanilla extract will be ready to use.

Vanilla salt Flavoured salts are all the rage, and very easy to make at home. Vanilla salt is very good sprinkled on fish or chicken, or over vegetable purées. And best of all, I think, it does wonders for a simple fried egg. Use the same method with other spices – cumin or fennel, for instance – or even with toasted sheets of dried nori (Japanese seaweed), broken into flakes.

For vanilla salt: Grind a vanilla pod to a powder in a spice grinder. Heat a medium frying pan over a moderate heat and add 50g flaky sea salt. Stir and shake the salt until it is very hot, then add the ground vanilla. Continue to shake and mix for another minute. Then tip the flavoured salt onto a cool plate or tray. Leave to cool, then store in an airtight jar.

vanilla ice cream

There's a good reason why vanilla ice cream is so popular: it is simply one of the greatest culinary creations ever. There's only one way to ensure that you get the full pleasure, and that's to make it yourself. Easy and impressive.

Serves 6

300ml full-cream milk

1 vanilla pod, slit open lengthways

3 large egg yolks

110g caster sugar

300ml double cream

Put the milk into a heavy-based saucepan with the vanilla pod and bring slowly up to the boil, stirring every now and then. Take off the heat, cover and leave to infuse in a warm place for 20–30 minutes.

Whisk the egg yolks and sugar together in a bowl, and then whisk in the milk, together with the vanilla pod. Set the bowl over a pan of lazily simmering water, making sure that the base of the bowl is not in contact with the water. Stir until the custard thickens enough to coat the back of the spoon. Leave to cool, then sieve to remove the vanilla pod and odd threads of egg white that might be lurking in there.

Whip the cream lightly and fold in the cooled custard. If you have an ice-cream maker, churn until thick, then serve or transfer to a suitable container and freeze until needed.

If you don't have an ice-cream maker, pour the mixture into a shallow container and pop into the freezer, set to its coldest setting. Leave until the mixture has set around the sides, then break up and push towards the centre of the container. Return to the freezer and leave until set but not yet solid. Scoop into the bowl of a processor and whiz quickly to smooth out coarse ice crystals. If you don't have a processor, flex your muscles and beat hard. Return to the freezer to set solid.

Transfer the ice cream to the fridge to soften about 45 minutes before eating. Scoop into glass dishes to serve. A spoonful of poached cherries (see page 203) won't go amiss...

pineapple blitz torte

Serves 8

Cake:

75g plain flour

1 level teaspoon baking powder

⅛ teaspoon salt

110g softened butter

110g caster sugar

4 large egg yolks

about 70–80ml milk

1 teaspoon vanilla extract

Meringue:

4 large egg whites

125g caster sugar

1 teaspoon vanilla extract

60g flaked almonds

Filling:

250ml double cream

1 tablespoon icing sugar

½ teaspoon vanilla extract

250g drained weight canned pineapple, chopped, or fresh pineapple (see below)

In her Fruit Book, my mother Jane Grigson described this recipe as 'a splendid pineapple cake' and indeed it is, with its layers of sponge, meringue and cream, all sharpened with flashes of pineapple.

The method seems peculiar, but don't panic that the cake layers are disturbingly thin, or that they come out of the oven when they are not quite cooked. It all works beautifully in the end.

Start with the cake. Preheat the oven to 160°C/Gas mark 3. Base-line two 20cm sandwich tins with baking parchment and grease the sides.

Mix the flour with the baking powder and salt; set aside. In a bowl, cream the butter with the sugar until light and fluffy. Beat in one of the egg yolks followed by a heaped tablespoon of flour. Repeat until all 4 egg yolks are incorporated, then start alternating slurps of milk with flour until the flour is all used up. Add a little more milk if necessary to produce a batter with a dropping consistency. Beat in the vanilla extract. Divide the mixture between the two tins and bake for 15 minutes.

Meanwhile, tackle the meringue. Whisk the egg whites in a clean bowl until stiff, then whisk in the sugar, a tablespoon at a time. Keep whisking until the meringue is thick and glossy. Whisk in the vanilla extract.

Take the two cakes from the oven and pile the meringue on top of them, smoothing it down lightly, then roughing up the surface here and there to give a bit of character. Scatter flaked almonds over the better-looking one, and swiftly return to the oven for another 15 minutes. Leave to cool in the tins.

To make the filling, whisk the cream with the icing sugar and vanilla extract until thick.

Place the cake without almonds, meringue side down, on a serving plate. Spread the cream thickly over it, then scatter with pineapple. Cover with the other cake, almond and meringue side up. The cake is ready to devour.

NOTE Fresh pineapple is nicest if you are eating the cake immediately, but it will react with the cream after half an hour or so, developing a bitter taste. Safer to use either tinned pineapple, or to poach fresh pineapple in a sugar syrup with a vanilla pod for 5 minutes, then leave to cool before layering up.

amish vanilla pie

Serves 8

Pastry:

250g plain flour

pinch of salt

1 heaped tablespoon icing sugar

125g chilled unsalted butter, diced

1 large egg, lightly beaten

about 1 tablespoon water

Filling:

120g light muscovado sugar

1 level tablespoon flour

4 tablespoons black treacle

1½ teaspoons vanilla extract

1 large egg, beaten

225ml water

Crumble topping:

150g plain flour

120g light muscovado sugar

1 teaspoon baking powder

generous pinch of salt

60g chilled unsalted butter, diced

The American Amish community is known for its simple, old-fashioned delicious cooking, and this tart is a perfect example. The sweetness of the filling is balanced by the dark liquorice flavour of molasses or black treacle and the softer waft of vanilla, and the biscuity crumble layer on top is a lovely contrast. Highly recommended.

To make the pastry, mix the flour, salt and icing sugar together in a bowl and rub in the butter until the mixture resembles coarse breadcrumbs. Add the egg and just enough water to form a soft dough. Knead briefly to smooth out, then wrap in cling film and chill in the fridge for half an hour.

Roll out the pastry on a lightly floured board, then use to line a 23cm tart tin with removable base. Prick the base lightly with a fork all over, then chill while you make the filling and topping.

For the crumble topping, mix together the flour, sugar, baking powder and salt, then rub in the butter until the mixture resembles fine breadcrumbs. Place in the fridge until needed.

Now the filling proper. Put the sugar, flour, treacle, vanilla and egg into a bowl and whisk together, gradually adding the water. Tip into a saucepan and bring to the boil over a medium heat, stirring constantly. Set aside to cool.

Preheat the oven to 180°C/Gas mark 4. Pour the cooled treacle mixture into the pastry case (no need to pre-bake), then sprinkle the crumble topping evenly over the top. Bake for 35–40 minutes, until golden brown. Serve warm or at room temperature, with cream.

crème chantilly

Serves 6

300ml whipping or double cream

1 tablespoon icing sugar

1 teaspoon vanilla extract

A classic accompaniment to all manner of puddings, Crème Chantilly is equally good with meringues, or a hot apple pie, or a fudgy chocolate cake. It's a simple, joyful amalgam of whipped cream, sugar and vanilla. Quite how much sugar or vanilla is open to debate. Be influenced by the pudding in question. If it is very sweet, go easy on the sugar, if the flavour is delicate, practise restraint with the vanilla.

And if you fancy a change, give mascarpone the same treatment, though of course, you won't need to whip it, just beat in sugar and vanilla extract until evenly mixed.

Put all the ingredients in a bowl and whisk until the cream is just thick enough to hold its shape softly. Taste and add more sugar or vanilla if you wish. Spoon into a serving bowl, cover and refrigerate until needed.

There are so very many spice blends around the world that it would be impossible to include them all in one small book. I make no apology for singling out just ten of the finest. These are the spice blends that I use frequently, with constant relish. You can buy most of them ready blended, smoothly ground and seemingly perfect, but they will never have the impact of the spices you grind and mix for yourself at home. Most spice blends vary to some extent, but the first four have a more or less definitive list of ingredients.

spice blends

dhana jeera
quatre épices
chinese five-spice powder
japanese seven-spice
za'atar
panch phoron
sri lankan roasted curry powder
mixed spice
ras-el-hanout
garam masala

dhana jeera

Simply a mixture of cumin (jeera) and coriander (dhana), this is used widely in West India. To make it, mix 2 parts coriander seeds with one part cumin seeds. Dry-fry, then cool and grind to a powder. Store in an airtight container if not using immediately.

Using dhana jeera

This is a powerful double-act and can be used to rev up an endless number of recipes. Obviously, it can be added to all kinds of curries and other stews. It is also excellent sprinkled on fish, or salads, or mashed with softened butter to make a flavoured butter for a juicy steak.

quatre épices

From France, though also enjoyed in the Middle East, quatre épices is a tingling blend of pepper, cloves, nutmeg and ginger, usually made from the raw spices.

2 tablespoons peppercorns (black or white)
1 tablespoon cloves
1 tablespoon freshly grated nutmeg
1 tablespoon ground ginger

Grind the pepper and cloves to a powder and mix with the nutmeg and ginger. Store in an airtight container.

Using quatre épices

This is a brilliant everyday spice mix that gives a massive boost to all kinds of savoury dishes. It is widely used in charcuterie, particularly sausages, salamis and pâtés, as well as in stews, vegetable dishes and more.

chinese five-spice powder

A wonderfully energetic and distinctive blend of star anise, cinnamon (or cassia), Szechuan pepper, fennel seeds and ginger.

1 tablespoon Szechuan peppercorns
4 whole star anise, broken into segments
2 cinnamon sticks (each 7–8cm), broken into pieces
1 teaspoon fennel seeds
1 tablespoon ground ginger

Dry-fry the peppercorns, star anise segments, cinnamon sticks and fennel seeds. Allow to cool. Grind to a powder, sift to remove splinters and lumps, then mix with the ginger. Store in an airtight jar.

Using chinese five-spice powder

Although good with all kinds of foods, this spice blend is particularly effective with fatty meats such as pork, duck or goose. It is a key ingredient in Char siu pork, but for a quicker appreciation of the taste, rub it over duck breasts or pork chops before cooking.

japanese seven-spice

Known as Shichimi Togarashi, this citrus-scented blend – perfumed with dried tangerine zest – is often used to give elegantly displayed morsels a final flourish. Literally 'seven-flavour chilli', this is no shrinking violet.

3 teaspoons Szechuan peppercorns
2 teaspoons white sesame seeds
2 teaspoons black sesame seeds
4 dried hot chillies
dried zest of 1 tangerine
1 teaspoon ground dried nori (seaweed)
1 teaspoon black poppy seeds

Dry-fry the Szechuan peppercorns and sesame seeds, adding the chillies towards the end. Grind to a coarse powder together with the tangerine zest and nori. Mix in the poppy seeds. Store in an airtight container.

Using japanese seven-spice

Sprinkle over a humble fried egg to transform breakfast into a bold event. More traditionally, use it in soups and with noodles or rice. It's also often sprinkled onto fish and other foods just before serving.

za'atar

Za'atar means many things. Firstly it is the name of several kinds of wild marjoram/thyme that grow across the Middle East, including the warm, slightly bitter hyssop. Secondly, and more relevant here, it is one of the most divine spice/herb blends ever.

For the real deal, you need to use za'atar in your za'atar. If this is not available, substitute either straight dried thyme, or dried wild thyme, or a mixture of dried thyme and oregano.

2 tablespoons ground sumac
2 tablespoons dried thyme
2 tablespoons toasted sesame seeds
1 teaspoon coarse salt

Grind the sumac, thyme, 1 tablespoon sesame seeds and salt to a rough powder; a spice grinder works better than a pestle and mortar here. Stir in the remaining sesame seeds. Store in an airtight jar.

Using za'atar

This is a sprinkling-on spice blend, rather than a mixing-in one. Possibly the most enticing use of all is on soft, puffy Lebanese flatbreads: mix the za'atar with a little olive oil to moisten and spread thickly on rounds of soft white dough before they go into a hot oven.

For virtually instant gratification, put the za'atar into a bowl; pour good olive oil into another. Dip hunks of fresh bread first in the oil, then in the spices, then pop into your mouth. Breadsticks, carrot sticks, strips of pepper, batons of cucumber – they all love za'atar.

Za'atar is also heavenly sprinkled over roast potato wedges, or grilled lamb or chicken.

panch phoron

Panch phoron literally means five spices, but don't for a minute think that this Bengali five-spice is anything like Chinese five-spice. It is a powerful blend of whole mustard, kalonji, cumin, fenugreek and fennel, giving a distinct character to the cooking of the region.

Equal quantities of:
Brown or black mustard seeds
Kalonji (nigella) seeds
Cumin seeds
Fenugreek seeds
Fennel seeds

Mix the spices. Store in an airtight container.

Using panch phoron

Usually the spices are tempered, whole, in hot oil, but if you want to use them in other ways, dry-fry them first, allow to cool, then crush coarsely.

Panch phoron is excellent with practically anything savoury – fish, meat, vegetables, potatoes, dahl, pickles and so on. Having said that, I have a particular fondness for potatoes or rice seasoned with panch phoron.

To make Bengali-style pilau rice, temper panch phoron in hot oil, add some onion, garlic and ginger and when patched with brown, stir in a little turmeric, then the rice. Mix well before adding twice the volume of water to rice, and some salt. Bring up to the boil, reduce the heat and cover tightly. Cook for 10 minutes, without stirring, by which time the rice will be tender, having absorbed all the liquid. Check the seasoning and serve.

To zip up leftover boiled potatoes, cut into chunks, then fry in hot oil until touched with brown. Add crushed panch phoron and salt and cook for a few more minutes.

sri lankan roasted curry powder

Sri Lankan curry powders are hot and fragrant. This one stands out from the crowd for its distinctive toasty depth. The difference is that the whole spices are roasted to within an inch of their life. The trick is to hold your nerve, and keep on shaking that pan, then whip it off the heat just before the spices burn. Be sure to have plenty of extra spices to hand, just in case the first batch carbonises.

1 tablespoon coriander seeds
1½ teaspoons cumin seeds
scant ¼ teaspoon fenugreek seeds
½ teaspoon fennel seeds
2.5cm piece cinnamon stick
3 cloves
5 green cardamom pods
1 dried bay leaf
2 hot dried chillies

Heat a heavy-based frying pan over a moderate heat. Add all the ingredients except the bay leaf and chillies. Dry-fry, stirring constantly until all the spices are well browned. Now add the bay leaf and chillies, and continue stirring until these have started to brown too, and the other spices are an alarming dark mahogany brown, but don't let them burn. Tip into a bowl, cool for a few minutes, then grind to a powder. Allow to cool completely. Store in an airtight jar if not using immediately.

Using sri lankan roasted curry powder

Use this unique curry powder in the Sri Lankan cashew nut and pea curry (on page 73), or the Sri Lankan chicken curry (on page 185).

Of course you can use it in practically any curry you like, as long as you're looking for more than a delicate hint of spice.

Since the spices are all roasted, you can also use this curry powder in the same way as you would garam masala. In other words, stir it into curries, or soups or sauces just before serving to give them a last-minute lift.

mixed spice

British mixed spice is a comforting, sweet spice blend, used in traditional baking. There's no exact formula, and the spices vary from one version to another, but nutmeg, cinnamon, cloves and coriander are nearly always included. Allspice, ginger, cardamom, caraway, mace and pepper may also get a look in. British mixed spice is akin to American pumpkin pie spice mix, which usually consists of nutmeg, cinnamon, cloves and ginger.

I love the neatness of this old mixed spice recipe.
Grind your own spices to get the full impact:

6 teaspoons ground coriander
5 teaspoons ground cinnamon
4 teaspoons ground allspice
3 teaspoons ground nutmeg
2 teaspoons ground ginger
1 teaspoon ground cloves

Mix the ground spices together in a bowl, then store in an airtight container if not using immediately.

This is an alternative, more balanced version:

1 tablespoon whole allspice
1 cinnamon stick (7–8cm)
1 teaspoon cloves
1 tablespoon coriander seeds
1 nutmeg, freshly grated
2 tsp ground ginger

Grind the allspice, cinnamon, cloves and coriander seeds to a fine powder in an electric spice grinder. Stir in the nutmeg and ginger. Store in an airtight container unless using immediately.

Using mixed spice
Mixed spice adds warmth to cakes, biscuits, Christmas puddings and spicy Easter hot cross buns. It is excellent with apples and other cooked fruit. Try it mashed with butter and sugar in baked apples, or sprinkled over the filling of a blackberry and apple pie, or in a blueberry compote.

ras-el-hanout

Ras-el-hanout literally means 'top of the shop', and offers any Moroccan spice merchant the chance to show off the best of their wares. There is no set recipe, but it should emerge as a rather wonderful, very fragrant, mildly hot powder. If you want to buy it whilst on holiday, find a spice shop where they mix their own whole spice version and grind it to order, in front of you.

Your average ras-el-hanout contains anywhere between 20 and 50 spices but some, reputedly, may pack in as many as a hundred. So, the up-shot of this is that you can create your own version at home, although it is unlikely to taste like any you will find in Morocco. On the other hand, neither do most of the ready-made ras-el-hanouts sold outside North Africa.

Here's one possible way to go on your very own top-of-the-shop:

Roughly equal quantities of:
Coriander seeds
Cumin seeds
Black peppercorns
Allspice
Cinnamon stick
Caraway seeds
Green cardamom pods
Dried red chillies
Dried rosebuds
Dried lavender flowers
Ground ginger
Ground nutmeg
Ground turmeric

Dry-fry the whole spices in a wide frying pan over a medium heat, adding the cardamom and chillies just as the other spices are nearly toasted. Tip into a bowl and leave to cool. Grind to a powder with the rosebuds and lavender, then stir in the ground spices. Store in an airtight jar.

Using ras-el-hanout

Somehow this anarchic free-for-all of a spice mix blends into a smooth, beautifully balanced ingredient. You can simply use it as a rub on meat or fish, together with a little salt and olive oil, before grilling, barbecuing or roasting in a hot oven. Or mix it in with rice in a pilau, or in minced meat dishes (such as the kofta on page 68). Work it in tagines, tomato sauces and soups, or try it on vegetables, drizzled with melted butter or olive oil first. In all of these instances be cautious at first (you just can't tell how strong it's going to taste), adding more as required.

garam masala

It's impossible to give an exact definition of garam masala. 'Garam' means hot and 'masala' means nothing more than a mixture of spices, but hot in this case does not mean as in chillies or pepper. No, it means deep and warm and powerful, and really the point of any garam masala is to big up the flavour of a dish so that it buzzes.

Mostly garam masala is added to food shortly before serving so that its flavour is at its peak of energy. However, I've come across recipes where it goes into the pan in the early stages of cooking. I also thought this was always a ground spice mix, but now I find that garam masala can be made up of whole spices.

The biggest confusion of all: every region and practically every cook within it has their own definitive version of garam masala. Not only that, but many commercial garam masalas are poor replicas of any of the genuine articles, as they bulk them out with a disproportionate percentage of the cheaper spices.

The only answer, I think, is to make your very own personalised garam masala, full of divine, warm, full scent. Use the formula below as your starting point, and have fun with it.

1 teaspoon cloves
2 teaspoons black peppercorns
1 tablespoon coriander seeds
2 teaspoons cumin seeds
1 cinnamon stick (about 8cm)
seeds from 15 green cardamom pods
½ nutmeg, freshly grated
1 dried bay leaf

Dry-fry the cloves, peppercorns, coriander and cumin seeds, and cinnamon stick. Tip into a bowl and leave to cool. Grind to a powder with the remaining ingredients. Store in an airtight jar.

Using garam masala
Anything goes, it seems. Principally, however, this spice mix is designed to go into curries or soups right at the end of the cooking period. It works with chicken, beef, lamb, with pulses of all sorts, and with vegetables too.

SPICEMONGERS

Most supermarkets and delis sell a decent range of spices, many of which are fair-trade, but if you want organic spices or something out of the ordinary, or you want the ultimate quality, you will have to turn to the specialists.

The Spice Shop
1 Blenheim Crescent
London W11 2EE
www.thespiceshop.co.uk
0207 221 4448
Possibly the most comprehensive spice shop in the world, certainly the most crowded. This tiny cavern is packed to the hilt with every spice you've ever heard of and many that you haven't. If you can't get to London, order online.

Seasoned Pioneers
www.seasonedpioneers.co.uk
0800 0682348
Seasoned Pioneers have brought many hard-to-get spices and fabulous spice blends to delis and supermarkets. The quality is impeccable. If there isn't a stockist near you, buy online.

Steenbergs
www.steenbergs.co.uk
01765 640088
Handsomely packaged, high-quality organic spices from all corners of the world. Occasionally stocked in delis, but they offer a swift and efficient online service.

Bart Spices
www.bartspices.com
0117 977 3474
Bart Spices are now a common sight on supermarket shelves, but more intriguing products can be found on their website, including the wonderful spices and teas from the POABS biodynamic estate in Kerala.

Peppers by Post
www.peppersbypost.biz
www.seaspringseeds.co.uk
www.seaspringplants.co.uk
01308 897766
01308 897898
These all lead to Joy and Michael Michaud, who have been growing chillies by the sea in Dorset for decades. They are responsible for the Dorset Naga, one of the hottest chillies in the world. Buy seeds, plants or whole fresh chillies.

Cool Chile
www.coolchile.co.uk
0870 9021145
This is the site to turn to for all things Mexican, including a brilliant rostrum of Mexican chillies – whole, powdered, *en adobo* and more.

REFERENCE

WEBSITES

www.uni-graz.at
Gernot Katzer is a thermochemist
with a total passion for spices.
This is where I turn first when I
want solid, fascinating unadorned
information on any spice.

www.theepicentre.com
An excellent general guide to spices.

www.fao.org
The Food and Agriculture
Organisation of the United Nations
is full of facts and figures on
agricultural practices around
the world.

www.indianspices.com
The website for the Government
of India Spices Board.

www.plantcultures.org
This website emerges from one of
the greatest botanical gardens –
Kew Gardens in London.

www.nrcss.org/index.asp
National Research Centre on Seed
Spices, Indian Council of Agricultural
Research, Rajasthan.

www.prota.org
Website of Plant Resources of
Tropical Africa.

BOOKS

Herbs, Spices and Flavourings,
Tom Stobart (Grub Street 1998)

Spice Crops, E. A. Weiss
(Wallingford: CABI Publishing 2002)

The New Guide To Spices,
Sallie Morris (Hermes House 1998)

The Complete Book of Spices,
Jill Norman (Dorling Kindersley,
1990)

Ultimate Curry Bible,
Madhur Jaffrey (Ebury Press, 2003)

Flavours of India,
Madhur Jaffrey (BBC Books, 1995)

A New Book of Middle Eastern Food,
Claudia Roden (Penguin, 1968)

*Spices, Salt and Aromatics in the
English Kitchen,*
Elizabeth David (Penguin, 1970)

Nathaniel's Nutmeg, Giles Milton,
(Hodder and Stoughton, 1999)

Pepper, Christine McFadden
(Absolute Press, 2008)

ACKNOWLEDGEMENTS

I've enjoyed writing this book hugely, and not only because of the subject. I'd like to thank Jane O'Shea at Quadrille for making it possible in the first place, and for giving me the impetus to throw myself into the subject head first; her enthusiasm has buoyed me up. Janet Illsley has been a joy to work with, nudging gently when necessary, providing a knowledgeable springboard, and keeping a keen eye on the flow of pages and the balance of recipes. I've been thrilled to see my vague ideas of how I wanted the book to look transformed with admirable speed into a bright, clean energetic design by Gabriella Le Grazie.

The photography team is decidedly starry, with the brilliant Anna Jones transforming my recipes into visual feasts, and the eminent photographer David Loftus transforming these into stunning, edible photos.

I'd like to say a massive thank you to my agent, Borra Garson for conjuring a deal out of thin air, and to Emma, Kate and the rest of the team for keeping other balls rolling.

Back in Oxford, I've been helped out in so many ways by Jennine Hughes, a rock if ever there was one. And by lovely Maggie, whose uncle makes the best sausages in Poland. Florrie and Sid have not grumbled too much when they've had to walk the dog, or make themselves lunch yet again. Most of the book has been written in my new office, known to the wider world as the Summertown Wine Café. Thank you all: Valère, JP, François, Enoma, Lucy, Megan, Rob, Monique, Tom, Will, Josie and all the rest of the gang.

Publishing director Jane O'Shea
Creative director Helen Lewis
Project editor Janet Illsley
Art direction & design Gabriella Le Grazie
Photographer David Loftus
Food & props stylist Anna Jones, assisted by Emily Ezekiel
Production Aysun Hughes, Vincent Smith

First published in 2011 by
Quadrille Publishing Limited
Alhambra House, 27–31 Charing Cross Road, London WC2H 0LS
www.quadrille.co.uk

Text © 2011 Sophie Grigson
Photography © 2011 David Loftus
Design and layout © 2011 Quadrille Publishing Limited
The rights of the author have been asserted.

Cataloguing in Publication Data: a catalogue record for this book is available from the British Library.

ISBN 978 184949 0344

Printed in China